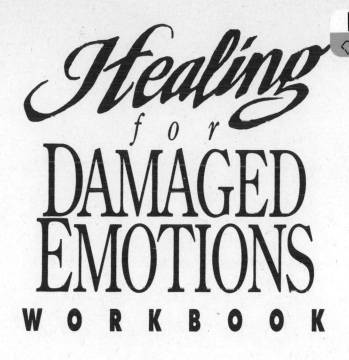

Healing
f o r
DAMAGED EMOTIONS
W O R K B O O K

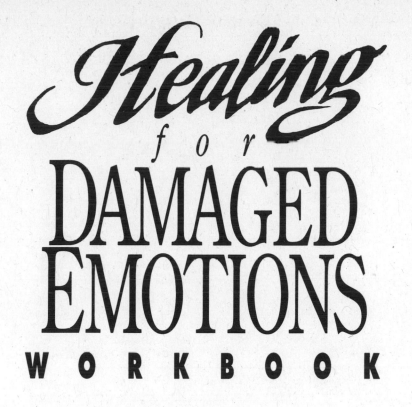

Healing
for
DAMAGED EMOTIONS
WORKBOOK

A Recovery Workbook for
Healing for Damaged Emotions

David A. Seamands
and Beth Funk

David C Cook®

transforming lives together

Other Books by David Seamands

Freedom From the Performance Trap
Healing for Damaged Emotions
Healing Meditations for Life
Healing of Memories
If Only
Putting Away Childish Things
Putting Away Childish Things Workbook

HEALING FOR DAMAGED EMOTIONS WORKBOOK
Published by David C. Cook
4050 Lee Vance View
Colorado Springs, CO 80918 U.S.A.

David C. Cook Distribution Canada
55 Woodslee Avenue, Paris, Ontario, Canada N3L 3E5

David C. Cook U.K., Kingsway Communications
Eastbourne, East Sussex BN23 6NT, England

David C. Cook and the graphic circle C logo
are registered trademarks of Cook Communications Ministries.

Unless otherwise noted, Scripture quotations are taken from the King James Version of the Bible. (Public Domain); NASB are taken from the New American Standard Bible, © Copyright 1960, 1995 by The Lockman Foundation. Used by permission; PH are taken from J.B. Phillips: The New Testament in Modern English, revised editions © J.B. Phillips, 1958, 1960, 1972, permission of Macmillan Publishing Co. and Collins Publishers; MLB are taken from the Modern Language Bible: The Berkeley Version in Modern English, © 1945, 1959, 1969 by Zondervan. Used by permission; NCV are taken from the New Century Version®. Copyright © 1987, 1988, 1991 by Thomas Nelson. Used by permission. All rights reserved; NIV are taken from the Holy Bible, New International Version®. NIV®. Copyright © 1973, 1978, 1984 by International Bible Society. Used by permission of Zondervan. All rights reserved.

Recommended Dewey Decimal Classification: 200.19 or 152.92
Suggested Subject Headings: CHRISTIAN LIVING; RECOVERY
ISBN 978-1-56476-025-8

© 2001 by SP Publications, Inc.
© 2004 by Cook Communications Ministries

Cover Photography: © Kevin Muggleton/Corbisstockmarket

Printed in the United States of America
First Edition 2001

21 22 23 24 25 26

080411

CONTENTS

Foreword 7
Preface 9
Introduction 11

PART ONE

1. Damaged Emotions 17
2. Guilt, Grace, and Debt-Collecting 37
3. The Wounded Healer 55
4. Satan's Deadliest Weapon 67
5. Healing Our Low Self-Esteem—Part 1 81
6. Healing Our Low Self-Esteem—Part 2 93
7. Symptoms of Perfectionism 105
8. The Process of Healing for Perfectionism 119
9. Super You or Real You? 137
10. Myths and Truths about Depression 151
11. Dealing with Depression 165
12. Healed Helpers 179

PART TWO

Appendix One
    Group Study Format 197
    Guidelines for Group Sharing 200
    Personal Journey Summary Sheets 201
Appendix Two
    Support Group Resources 227
    Specialized Reading Resources 229
Appendix Three
    Supplemental Journaling Pages 233

FOREWORD

When the healing of memories became a popular topic several years ago, a psychologist friend gave me some good advice: "Listen to the tape by David Seamands. It's concise, biblical, and the clearest statement that anyone has given on this topic."

Now Dr. Seamands has expanded his earlier ideas into a book which blends clear biblical theology, solid psychology, and practical common sense. The author writes about anger, guilt, depression, inferiority, and perfectionism—that constant and all-pervading feeling that we are never "good enough." Then he takes us to the heart of lingering emotional pain and shows how we can find permanent freedom from our inner turmoil and damaged feelings.

This book avoids simplistic answers, pious condemnation, and confusing jargon. Instead, Dr. Seamands writes with compassion, graciousness, and understanding, all interspersed with bright humor and warm anecdotes about real people. Here is the gentle sharing of a sensitive pastor who is equally at ease in imparting biblical truths and in counseling troubled and searching people.

Because I deeply respect David Seamands' many abilities, I approached his book with high expectations. I did not come away disappointed. His book proved to be interesting, informative, and personally helpful. I am grateful to have the privilege of enthusiastically recommending the following pages.

Gary R. Collins, Ph.D.
Professor and Chairman,
Division of Pastoral Counseling and Psychology
Trinity Evangelical Divinity School

PREFACE

Early in my pastoral experience, I discovered that I was failing to help two groups of people through the regular ministries of the church. Their problems were not being solved by the preaching of the Word, commitment to Christ, the filling of the Spirit, prayer, or the Sacraments.

I saw one group being driven into futility and loss of confidence in God's power. While they desperately prayed, their prayers about personal problems didn't seem to be answered. They tried every Christian discipline, but with no result. As they played the same old cracked record of their defeats, the needle would get stuck in repetitive emotional patterns. While they kept up the outward observances of praying and paying and professing, they were going deeper and deeper into disillusionment and despair.

I saw the other group moving toward phoniness. These people were repressing their inner feelings and denying to themselves that anything was seriously wrong, because "Christians can't have such problems." Instead of facing their problems, they covered them with a veneer of Scripture verses, theological terms, and unrealistic platitudes.

The denied problems went underground, only to later reappear in all manner of illnesses, eccentricities, terribly unhappy marriages, and sometimes even in the emotional destruction of their children.

During this time of discovery, God showed me that the ordinary ways of ministering would never help some problems. And He began to enable me to open up my own heart to personal self-discovery, and to new depths of healing love through my marriage, my children, and intimate friends.

God then led me to enlarge my pastoral ministry to include special care and prayer for damaged emotions and unhealed memories.

In the twenty years that I have been preaching, teaching, counseling, and distributing tapes on this subject, I have heard from thousands of formerly defeated Christians who have found release from emotional hangups and who have experienced the healing of crippling memories of the past.

In this book, you will meet some of those people. You will read of attitudes and feelings that are familiar to you or to someone dear to you.

Any resemblance to real persons is completely intentional. All of the people in this book are very much alive; their stories are used with permission. Names and locations have been changed to protect their confidence.

Any resemblance to your life may seem coincidental, but it is also intentional. For most of us have the same needs and longings.

I pray that these chapters will be helpful in picturing God's ways of repairing damaged emotions, of recycling hangups into wholeness, and of transforming crippled Christians into healed helpers.

David A. Seamands
The Methodist Parsonage
Wilmore, Kentucky

INTRODUCTION

Today many Christians struggle with emotional pain that is deeply rooted in the past. This unresolved pain manifests itself in "over-extended" patterns of living. We OVERwork, OVEReat, OVERcommit, OVERspend, OVERspiritualize, and OVERobsess about love and sex. A host of book titles, such as, *We Are Driven, Hiding from Love, How to Balance Time Demands, Help Lord—My Whole Life Hurts*, and *Imperative People*, reflect all too well the tenor of our uptight, on-the-edge approach to life. And Christians are not exempt. We must face the reality of our pain-filled past if we are going to proceed through life in a healthy way. That is what this workbook is all about. It is designed to help you find your way back to a place of balance by giving you an opportunity to take an honest look at the painful experiences of your past that have left you emotionally scarred in the present.

What makes this workbook different from the original work of the same title is that you now have an opportunity to journal your way through the entire text of *Healing for Damaged Emotions*. Questions have been inserted into the text at key places to help you personalize and record your thoughts, feelings, and experiences along the way.

Journal writing is a time-honored practice that dates back as far as the confessions of St. Augustine and the spiritual diaries of the Quakers. This discipline can serve you well in your individual program of personal growth and healing as you remain open to the Holy Spirit's work in your life. No matter how damaged you have been, you have the choice of opening yourself up to God's love and healing power through the Holy Spirit. As you write down your thoughts and feelings in response to the questions asked throughout the text, the Holy Spirit will gently bring the truth about your past to light and "the truth will set you free" (John 8:32).

HOW EACH CHAPTER IS ORGANIZED

There are four basic elements included in every chapter of this workbook. They are:

■ **The entire text of *Healing for Damaged Emotions*.** This book was first published in 1981 and has helped hundreds of thousands of readers worldwide deal honestly and successfully with their inner hurts. It is possible that you have at one point or another already read this book. But don't let that stop you from going through it again— *Healing for Damaged Emotions* is a book well worth rereading.

■ **Personal Reflection.** Key questions and reflection exercises have been built into the text to help you filter the truth of the text through the grid of your own experience. Here is where much healing can take place. Application of truth to life leads to transformation. The merits of journaling have already been cited in the previous paragraphs. You will greatly benefit from this book by taking time to write down your answers in the space provided. If you are unable to answer a question as you work through the material the first time, move on. The goal is NOT to answer every question. The goal is to get in touch with as much truth as is possible for you. Remember: God does not violate us, invade us, force Himself upon us, or overtake us. As you remain open to Him, the Holy Spirit will gently affirm to you that God can be trusted. He does have your best interest at heart. So trust Him. He will guide you as you read and write your way through this workbook.

■ **Prayerful Reflection.** Prayer is both talking to and hearing from God. At the end of each chapter you will have an opportunity to tell God in writing how you feel about the things you have read. Exercise rigorous honesty with Him. Dare to entrust your deepest fears and secrets to Him. Then listen carefully to hear what He has to say. God will meet you at your place of need.

■ **Personal Renewal.** The final exercise in each chapter is a meditation or memorization activity. One way your life will be transformed is through the "renewing of your mind" (Rom. 12:2). The Bible is the primary source book God has given us for renewing our minds. Hear what the writer of Hebrews tells us about God's Word: "[It] is alive and working and is sharper than a double-edged sword. It cuts all the way into us, where the soul and the spirit are joined, to the center of our joints and bones. And it judges the thoughts and feelings in our hearts" (Heb. 4:12, NCV). Each Scripture in this section reflects a key truth the author writes about in the chapter. Meditate and memorize (wherever possible) the passages listed. God can use His Word to bring tremendous healing to your thoughts and feelings.

HOW TO USE THIS BOOK

Healing for Damaged Emotions Workbook presents a series of writing exercises and ideas for personal growth and development. This material is designed for use by individuals as well as groups. No matter what approach you take in using the material, there are some basic guidelines to follow.

Individual Study

Pace yourself through each chapter, taking whatever time you need to complete the Personal Reflection, Prayerful Reflection, and Personal Renewal exercises as you read. You may get through all of the exercises in one sitting, or you may choose to spread your writing out over a longer period of time. Be patient with yourself. Give yourself time to digest the content of each chapter and reflect on its meaning. Share what you are learning with someone you trust.

Do not feel obligated to complete every exercise. However, if you find yourself avoiding a particular exercise or chapter, take a good look at your resistance and then make a special effort to work in that area of the book. This may be precisely the chapter or exercise that can really begin to help you heal.

Write out your answers fully. Don't use just a word or short phrase, but write complete sentences and paragraphs. You will find that the process of writing will help you gain awareness and perspectives that you may not have known you had.

As you work the material in this book you may be surprised at the power of the feelings that come up as you write. Give yourself permission to feel your feelings. Denying your feelings will only slow down the healing process; acknowledging them will speed it up and bring about the emotional and spiritual healing you desire.

Group Study

We are broken in the context of relationship; and we are also healed within the scope of relationships. Though there is great value in working the exercises in this book individually, you will find that your healing process is enhanced and accelerated by the mutual support and encouragement that is found in a small group setting.

Appendix One of this workbook gives you complete guidelines for using this material in groups. There is a Personal Journey Summary Sheet provided for each chapter of the book, plus a "Telling My Story" page that should be used the first time the group meets together. The group material has been designed in such a way that it is virtually self-facilitating. If you can read, you can lead. The success of the group is not dependent on one individual. Rather, it is the combined efforts of and group members' mutual commitment to the group process that will bring about an emotionally and spiritually satisfying outcome. Group members will receive maximum benefit from the group process if they have taken time during the week to complete the writing exercises that are in Part 1 of the workbook.

Ideally, a group meeting should last one-and-a-half to two hours. Try to start and end each meeting on time. At your first meeting, communicate clearly the Guidelines for Group Sharing (also found in Appendix One). These guidelines will help provide a safe environment for group members. Safety is essential to the healing process. And confidentiality is essential to feeling safe. You will find additional facilitator helps in Appendix One at the back of this workbook to help you in your group process.

THE VALUE OF SUPPORT

Christ-centered and secular self-help support groups have flourished in the past decade. These groups strive to create a safe and nurturing environment where members can face and learn to effectively deal with the pain in their lives. It helps to know that someone else cares and is willing to share their experience, strength and hope with us along the way.

Solomon, in the Book of Ecclesiastes, had this to say about the value of supportive relationships: "Two are better than one, because they have a good return for their work: If one falls down, his friend can help him up. But pity the man who falls and has no one to help him up! . . . Though one may be overpowered, two can defend themselves. A cord of three strands is not quickly broken" (Ecc. 4:9-10, 12, NIV). Make a wise choice—employ the power of group dynamics to help you find healing for damaged emotions. You are not alone.

PART ONE

He Himself took our infirmities.

Matthew 8:17, NASB

Likewise the Spirit also helpeth our infirmities; for we know not what we should pray for as we ought; but the Spirit itself maketh intercession for us according to the will of God.

Romans 8:26-27

Chapter 1
Damaged Emotions

One Sunday evening in 1966, I preached a sermon called "The Holy Spirit and the Healing of Our Damaged Emotions." It was my first venture into this area, and I was convinced that God had given me that message, or I would never have had the courage to preach it. What I said that evening about the healing of memories and damaged emotions is now old hat. You will find it in a lot of books. But it wasn't old then.

When I got up to preach I looked down at the congregation and saw dear old Dr. Smith. Now Dr. Smith had been a very real part of my boyhood. When my wife, Helen, and I first heard that we were appointed to our present pastorate, a few elderly faces appeared in our minds to trouble us. Dr. Smith was one of them, for I wondered how I could ever minister to him. He had nearly scared the life out of me with his preaching when I was young, and I was still uneasy in his presence.

When I saw him in the congregation that evening, my heart sank. But I went ahead and preached the message that I felt God had given me. After the service, which was followed by a very wonderful time for many at the prayer altar, Dr. Smith remained seated in the congregation. I was busy praying with people at the altar; somewhere back in my mind, I was also praying that he would leave. He didn't. Finally, he came up to the altar, and in his own inimitably gruff way, he said, "David, may I see you in your office?"

All those images from the past arose and the frightened little boy inside of me followed the old man. As I sat down in my office, I felt somewhat like Moses must have before the fire and smoke of Sinai.

But I was wrong about him—I hadn't allowed for change. I had frozen him at one stage and hadn't let him grow.

Very kindly, Dr. Smith said to me, "David, I've never heard a sermon quite like that before, but I want to tell you something." His eyes got moist. He had been an outstanding evangelist and preacher for many years, and had won thousands to Christ. He was a truly great man; but as he looked back over his own ministry he said, "You know, there was always a group of people I could never help. They were sincere people. I believe many of them were Spirit-filled Christians. But they had problems. They brought these things to me and I tried to help. But no amount of advice, no amount of Scripture or prayer on their part ever seemed to bring them lasting deliverance."

Then he said, "I always felt guilty in my ministry, David. But I think you are onto something. Work on it, develop it. Please keep preaching it, for I believe what you have found is the answer."

When he rose to leave, *my* eyes were wet as I said, "Thank you, Doctor." But most of all, I was inwardly saying, "Thank You, God, for Your affirmation through this dear man."

PERSONAL REFLECTION

■ Do you identify with the person Dr. Smith described to Dr. Seamands in his office that day? In what way(s) have you, as a sincere, Spirit-filled Christian, struggled with problems that just don't seem to go away—in spite of godly advice you've received, Scriptures you've read, or petitions you've made to God in prayer? Briefly describe your struggle.

_____

_____

_____

_____

■ In what areas of your life do you struggle the most? List those areas specifically. Examples: I repeatedly find myself in relationships where people use me. I have a critical spirit toward other people. I am unable to control my sexual impulses. What feelings do you have as the result of struggling in these areas of your life?

_____

_____

Through fifteen years, as tapes have gone out all over the world, letters and testimonies have confirmed my belief that there is another realm of problems which requires a special kind of prayer and a deeper level of healing by the Spirit. Somewhere between our sins, on the one hand, and our sickness, on the other, lies an area the Scripture calls "infirmities."

We can explain this by an illustration from nature. If you visit the far West, you will see those beautiful giant sequoia and redwood trees. In most of the parks the naturalists can show you a cross section of a great tree they have cut, and point out that the rings of the tree reveal the developmental history, year by year. Here's a ring that represents a year when there was a terrible drought. Here's where the tree was struck by lightning. Here are some normal years of growth. This ring shows a forest fire that almost destroyed the tree. Here's another of savage blight and disease. All of this lies embedded in the heart of the tree, representing the autobiography of its growth.

And that's the way it is with us. Just a few minutes beneath the protective bark, the concealing, protective mask, are the recorded rings of our lives.

There are scars of ancient, painful hurts . . . as when a little boy rushed downstairs one Christmas dawn and discovered in his Christmas stocking a dirty old rock, put there to punish him for some trivial boyhood naughtiness. This scar has eaten away in him, causing all kinds of interpersonal difficulties.

Here is the discoloration of a tragic stain that muddied all of life . . . as years ago behind the barn, or in the haystack, or out in the woods, a big brother took a little sister and introduced her into the mysteries—no, the miseries of sex.

And here we see the pressure of a painful, repressed memory . . . of running after an alcoholic father who was about to kill the mother, and then of rushing for the butcher knife. Such scars have been buried in pain for so long that they are causing hurt and rage that are inexplicable. And these scars are not touched by conversion and sanctifying grace, or by the ordinary benefits of prayer.

In the rings of our thoughts and emotions, the record is there; the memories are recorded, and all are alive. And they directly and deeply affect our concepts, our feelings, our relationships. They affect the way we look at life and God, at others and ourselves.

PERSONAL REFLECTION

■ For many of us, uncovering the recorded memories of our past is very painful. And we will do almost anything to avoid pain. We'll dull it, ignore it, excuse it, bury it, eat it . . . we just don't want to have to feel it. But the truth is, healing begins at the point of pain. In what ways have you been avoiding the pain of your past? What do you most fear about having to get in touch with that pain?

_____

_____

_____

_____

_____

■ Spend a minute or two reflecting on the character of God. What part of His character brings the greatest sense of comfort and security to you?

_____

_____

_____

_____

_____

Hold on to that part of who God is as you complete the following journaling exercise.

INSTRUCTIONS: Going back as far as you can remember, record in the rings on page 21 any past experiences that cause you to feel a sense of hurt or sadness. Starting with the outer rings first, write a short statement describing your most recent painful experiences. Move to the smaller, inner rings, noting there any painful childhood experiences that come to mind (things that were said and done to you). Try to recall how old you were when each experience happened, making a note of it next to the statement describing the experience. *NOTE: At some point, it may be necessary to journal in more detail these experiences. Additional Personal Journal sheets have been provided in the back of this workbook for this purpose.*

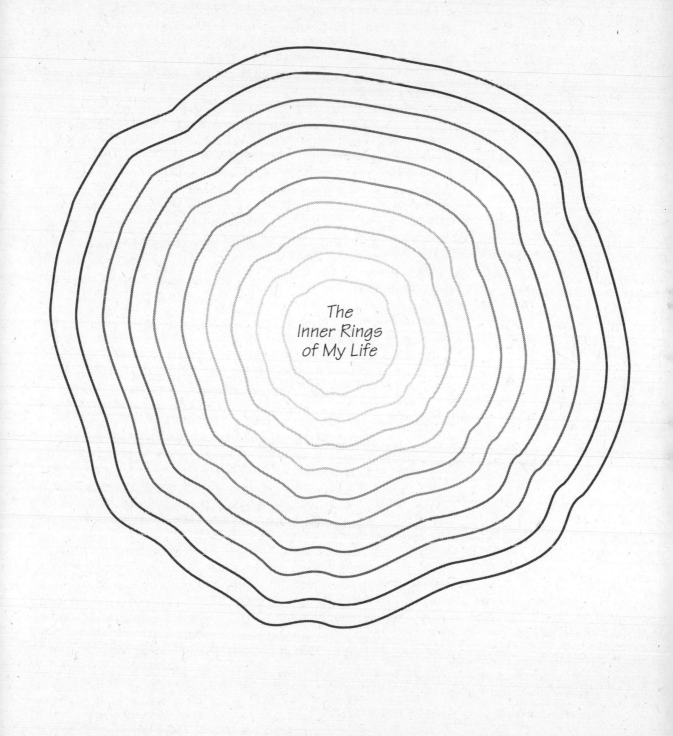

The
Inner Rings
of My Life

Preachers have often given people the mistaken idea that the new birth and being "filled with the Spirit" are going to automatically take care of their emotional hangups. But this just isn't true. A great crisis experience of Jesus Christ, as important and eternally valuable as this is, is not a shortcut to emotional health. It is not a quickie cure for personality problems.

It is necessary that we understand this, first of all, so that we can compassionately live with ourselves and allow the Holy Spirit to work with special healing in our own hurts and confusions. We also need to understand this in order to not judge other people too harshly, but to have patience with their confusing and contradictory behavior. In so doing, we will be kept from unfairly criticizing and judging fellow Christians. They're not fakes, phonies, or hypocrites. They are people, like you and me, with hurts and scars and wrong programming that interfere with their present behavior.

Understanding that salvation does not give instant emotional health offers us an important insight into the doctrine of sanctification. It is impossible to know how Christian a person is, merely on the basis of his outward behavior.

Isn't it true that by their fruits ye shall know them? (Matt. 7:16) Yes, but it is also true that by their roots you shall understand, and not judge them. Over here is John who may appear to be more spiritual and responsible as a Christian than Bill. But actually, considering John's roots and the good kind of soil he had to grow in and out of, Bill may be a saint by comparison. He may have made much more progress than John in really being conformed to the image of Jesus Christ. How wrong, how unchristian to superficially judge people!

Some may object: "What are you doing? Lowering standards? Are you denying the power of the Holy Spirit to heal our hangups? Are you trying to give us a copout for responsibility, so that we can blame life, or heredity, or parents, or teachers, or sweethearts, or mates for our defeats and failures? In the words of Paul: 'Shall we continue in sin, that grace may abound?'" (Rom. 6:1)

And I would answer as Paul answered that question, "God forbid!" What I am saying is that certain areas of our lives need special healing by the Holy Spirit. Because they are not subject to ordinary prayer, discipline, and willpower, they need a special kind of understanding, an unlearning of past wrong programming, and a relearning and reprogramming transformation by the renewal of our minds. And this is not done overnight by a crisis experience.

PERSONAL
REFLECTION

■ What objections, if any, do you find yourself raising subconsciously when you think about allowing the Holy Spirit to do a special healing work in your life at an emotional level? Try to put into words those messages you've been saying to yourself regarding your need for emotional healing. Can you isolate where those subconscious messages are coming from?

_____

_____

_____

_____

_____

Understanding that certain areas of our lives need special healing by the Holy Spirit will protect us from two extremes. Some Christians see anything that wiggles as the devil. Let me say a kind but firm word to young or immature Christians. Throughout the centuries the church has been very careful about declaring a person demon-possessed. There *is* such a thing as demon possession. On rare occasions, during my many years of ministry, I have felt led to take the authority of the name of Jesus to cast out what I believed was an evil spirit, and I have seen deliverance and healing.

But only careful, prayerful, mature, Spirit-filled Christians should ever attempt anything in the nature of exorcism. I spend a lot of time in the counseling room, picking up the pieces of people who have been utterly disillusioned and devastated, because immature Christians tried to cast imaginary demons out of them.

The other extreme is an overly simplistic pat-answer syndrome, which says, "Read your Bible. Pray. Have more faith. If you were spiritually OK, you wouldn't have this hangup. You would never get depressed. You would never have any sexual compulsions or problems."

However, people who say such things are being very cruel. They are only piling more weights on a person who is in pain and unsuccessfully struggling with an emotionally rooted problem. He already feels guilty about it; when people make him feel worse for even having the problem, they double the weight of his guilt and despair.

Perhaps you have heard about the man who was traveling on a dinner flight. When he opened his prepackaged meal, right on top of the salad he saw an enormous roach. When he got home he wrote an indignant letter to the president of the airline. A few days later, a special delivery letter came from the president. He was all apologies. "This was very unusual, but don't worry. I want to assure you that that particular airplane has been completely fumigated. In fact, all the seats and the upholstery have been stripped out. We have taken disciplinary action against the stewardess who served you that meal, and she may even be fired. It is highly probable that this particular aircraft will be taken out of service. I can assure you that it will never happen again. And I trust you will continue to fly with us."

Well, the man was terrifically impressed by such a letter, until he noticed something. Quite by accident the letter he had written had stuck to the back of the president's letter. When he looked at his own letter, he saw a note at the bottom that said, "Reply with the regular roach letter."

So often we reply with the regular roach letter to people suffering with emotional problems. We give pat, oversimplified answers, which drive them to deeper despair and disillusionment.

So, what are some of these damaged emotions? One of the most common is a deep *sense of unworthiness*, a continuous feeling of anxiety, inadequacy, and inferiority, an inner nagging that says, "I'm no good. I'll never amount to anything. No one could ever possibly love me. Everything I do is wrong."

What happens to this kind of person, when he becomes a Christian? Part of his mind believes in God's love, accepts God's forgiveness, and feels at peace for a while. Then, all of a sudden, everything within him rises up to cry out, "It's a lie! Don't believe it! Don't pray! There's no one up there to hear you. No one really cares. There's no one to relieve your anxiety. How could God possibly love you and forgive someone like you? You're too bad!"

What has happened? The good news of the Gospel has not penetrated down into his damaged inner self, which also needs to be evangelized. His deep inner scars must be touched and healed by the Balm of Gilead.

Then there's another kind of damaged emotions. For want of a better term, I call this the *perfectionist complex.* This is the inner feeling that says, "I can never quite achieve. I never do anything well enough. I can't please myself, others, or God." This kind of a person is always groping, striving, usually feeling guilty, driven by inner oughts and shoulds. "I ought to be able to do this. I should be able to do that. I must be a little bit better." He's ever climbing, but never reaching.

What happens to this person, when he becomes a Christian? Tragically enough, he usually transfers his perfectionism into his relationship with God, who is seen now as a figure on top of a tall ladder. He says to himself, "I'm going to climb up to God now. I'm His child, and I want to please Him, more than I want anything else."

So he starts climbing, rung by rung, working so hard, until his knuckles are bleeding and his shins are bruised. Finally, he reaches the top, only to find that his God has moved up three rungs; so he puts on his Avis button and determines to try a little harder. He climbs and struggles, but when he gets up there, his God has gone up another three rungs.

Some years ago I received a telephone call from the wife of a minister friend of mine, asking me to council her husband who had just suffered a complete nervous break down. As we were driving to the hospital, she began to talk about him. "I just don't understand Bill. It's almost as if he has a built-in slave drive that won't let him go. He can't relax, can't let down. He's always overworking. His people just love him; and they would do anything for him, but he can't let them. He's gone on and on like this for so many years that finally he has broken completely."

I began to visit with Bill, and after he was well enough to talk, he shared with me about his home and childhood. As Bill grew up he wanted very much to please his parents. He tried to win his mother's approval by occasionally helping her set the table. But she'd say, "Bill, you've got the knives in the wrong place." So he would put the knives in the right place. "Now you've got the forks wrong." After that it would be the salad plates. He could never please her. Try as hard as he might, he could never please his father either. He brought home his report card with B's and C's. His dad looked at the card and said, "Bill, I think if you try, you could surely get all B's, couldn' t you?" So he studied harder and harder, until one day he brought home all B's. Dad said, "But surely, you know, if you just put a little more effort into it, you could get all A's." So he worked and struggled through a semester or two, until finally he got all A's. He was so excited—now his Mother and Dad would surely be pleased with him. He ran home, for he could hardly wait. Dad looked at the report card and said, "Well, I know these teachers. They always give A's."

When Bill became a minister, all he did was exchange one mother and father for several hundred of them: His congregation became his unpleaseable parents. He could never satisfy them, no matter what he did. Finally, he just collapsed under the sheer weight of struggling for approval and trying to prove himself.

A famous God-is-dead theologian was being interviewed. The reporter asked, "Who do you mean by *God*?"

"God? God, to me, is that little inner voice that always says, 'That's not quite good enough.'"

He didn't tell us much about God, but he did say a lot about his own damaged personality. And I presume that such sick people produce sick theologies. Oh how the perfectionist complex defeats people in the Christian life! And how it even keeps people out of the kingdom!

PERSONAL REFLECTION

■ Do you see yourself as a person who struggles with a deep sense of unworthiness (inferiority) or as a perfectionist? Go back and read through the paragraphs which describe these two types of damaged emotions. As you read, underline or highlight any phrases or words that you relate to at a personal level. Complete this exercise before moving on to the next question.

■ At the heart of inferiority lies shame—the feeling that "I am not enough." A shame-based person finds it difficult to distinguish between these two realities: "I made a mistake and I am a mistake." Can you think of any instances when you've "beat yourself up" verbally because you made a mistake and felt ashamed of it? Give one or two examples, recording as many details about the situation as you can. Describe what happened, how you responded, and the feelings you experienced as the result of what happened.

_____

_____

_____

_____

■ Shame separates us from others, from God, and from ourselves. A.W. Tozer once said, "Most of us developed our concepts and feelings about our Heavenly Father from our earthly mothers and fathers, and these feelings become intertwined and confused. But the guilty and contradictory feelings are not the voice of God. They are often the continuing voice of Mother or Dad or Brother or Sister, or something internalized that puts pressure on us" (_The Knowledge of the Holy_, Harper & Row, 1961, p. 9). What internalized messages from the past are disabling you in the present? Jot them down. How are these messages affecting what you believe about how God sees you?

_____

_____

_____

_____

■ The perfectionist is always groping, striving, usually feeling guilty, driven by the inner oughts and shoulds. In what ways are you like this?

_____

_____

_____

_____

■ Can you think of a time when you tried your hardest to please someone only to be met with disapproval at one level or another? Describe it.

_____

_____

_____

_____

■ In what ways, if any, have you transferred your perfectionism onto your relationship with God? Do you subconsciously view Him as a relentless slave driver who is out of reach or just waiting for you to mess up? Describe God as you know Him today.

_____

_____

_____

_____

There is a third kind of damaged emotion that we can call _supersensitivity_. The supersensitive person has usually been hurt deeply. He reached out for love and approval and affection, but instead he got the opposite, and has scars deep inside of him. Sometimes he sees things other people don't see, and tends to feel things other people don't feel.

One day I was walking down the street and saw supersensitive Charlie coming toward me. I usually give him a lot of attention, but that morning I was very busy so I just said, "Hi, Charlie. How are you?" and passed on by. When I got back to the office, a church member called me on the phone and asked, "Are you mad at Charlie?"

"Charlie who?"

"Well, you know, Charlie Olson."

"Why, no. I just saw him down the street." Then I suddenly realized that I hadn't given Charlie the appreciation and the affirmation I usually do, knowing he is supersensitive.

Did you hear about the man who was so supersensitive he had to stop going to football games? Every time the team got into a huddle, he thought they were talking about him.

Supersensitive people need a lot of approval. You can never quite give them enough. And sometimes they seem very insensitive. They have been hurt so badly that instead of becoming sensitive, they cover it by being hard, tough. They want to get even and hurt others. So quite unbeknown to them, they spend their lives pushing people around, hurting and dominating them. They use money or authority or position or sex or even sermons to hurt people. Does all this affect their Christian experience? Yes, very deeply.

Then there are the people who are filled with *fears*. Perhaps the greatest of them all is the fear of failure. These damaged persons are so afraid of losing the game of life that they have a simple way out— never get into the game; just sit on the sidelines. They say, "I don't like the rules," or, "I don't care for the referee." "The ball isn't quite round." "The goals are not right."

I remember some years ago talking with a salesman in a used car lot. As we looked out the showroom window, we saw a man who was going around kicking tires on the cars. He was also raising the hoods and banging the fenders. The salesman said disgustedly, "Look at the guy out there. He's a wheel-kicker. They are the bane of our existence. They come in here all the time, but never buy cars because they can't make up their minds. Now watch him out there. He's kicking the tires. He'll say the wheels are out of line. He'll listen to the motor and say, 'Hear that knock?' Nobody else can hear the knock, but he can hear it. Something is always wrong. He is afraid to choose; he can never make up his mind, so he always finds an excuse."

Life is filled with wheel-kickers, people who fear failure, fear making the wrong decision. What happens to such people as they approach the Christian life? Believing is a great risk; it's very hard. Decisions tear them up. Faith comes hard. Witnessing is difficult. Launching out in the Holy Spirit and really surrendering to God is almost a trauma. Discipline is difficult. Fearful people live on *if onlys:* "If only this or if only that, then I would be OK." But since the *if only* never comes to pass, they usually never accomplish what they would like to. The fearful are the defeated and the indecisive.

PERSONAL REFLECTION

■ Fear paralyzes. In what, if any, areas of your life has fear caused paralysis to such an extent that you repeatedly feel defeated and/or indecisive in those areas? Listed below are several areas of life. Identify any area where fear is a problem and write a statement or two explaining how fear is keeping you stuck in that area of life.

Relationships_____

_____

_____

Work_____

_____

_____

Spiritual Life_____

_____

_____

Finances _____

_____

_____

Physical Well-being _____

_____

_____

Education _____

_____

_____

Relaxation & Play_____

_____

_____

Sex_____

_____

_____

Family_____

_____

_____

The whole area of *sex* is intricately mixed in with all these others, but needs a special word said about it.

When the Apostle Paul wrote his first epistle to the Corinthians, he dealt with every imaginable kind of human problem, and some which are almost unimaginable. He talked about quarrels, party splits, court cases, property disputes, and various kinds of sexual difficulty, from incest to prostitution. He talked about premarital relations and marital relations and postmarital relations. He wrote about widowhood, divorce, vegetarianism, getting drunk at the Communion table, speaking in tongues, death and funerals, taking up offerings, and conducting an every-member canvass in the church!

But he began his letter by saying he was not going to know anything among them except "Jesus Christ, and Him crucified" (1 Cor. 2:2). This means our Gospel is most practical, and gets right down to where we live. Much of Paul's letter had to do with sexual problems.

Because we Americans have been weaned on indiscipline, indecency, and sensuality, we are living in a modern Corinth. In our society, it is very difficult for anyone to grow to young adulthood without suffering some damage in the sex department of his personality.

I'm thinking of scores of people who have come to me for help. I remember a lady who had heard me speak in her church and then drove 1,200 miles to talk with me. I remember a man who finally came into the office and said that he had driven eleven times around the church, getting up enough nerve to come and see me. Both of these people were genuine Christians, and both were struggling with problems of homosexuality.

I am thinking of a young lady in a distant university where I held a preaching mission. To this day I don't know what she looks like, for she kept her back turned to me and her coat pulled up around her face, as she sat in a corner, sobbing. Finally, she said, "I've got to share this with someone else before I explode." Then, still facing the corner, she told me the sad story which we hear more and more often these days, about a father who had treated her not as a daughter, but as a wife.

I am thinking of scores of young men and women who were fed a lot of false and harmful ideas by well-meaning but ignorant parents and preachers. Now they are unfit for marriage, unable to be husbands and wives who can live without fear, guilt, and shame. Damaged? Yes, badly damaged.

PERSONAL REFLECTION

■ In her book, *A Door of Hope*, author Jan Frank states that "incest is the biggest hidden problem in the church today." Unfortunately, some victims don't even recall the incidents of abuse. What did you learn about sex in your family of origin? Briefly describe what you were told, what you observed, or experienced in the sexual area as a child, youth, or young adult.

_____

_____

_____

_____

Does the Gospel have a message for these various kinds of emotionally damaged persons? If it doesn't, then we had better put a padlock on our church doors, quit playing Christianity, and shut up about our "good news."

Paul wrote to the Roman Christians about the Holy Spirit who *helps our infirmities* (Rom. 8:26). Many of the modern translations use *weaknesses* or *cripplings* in place of the word *infirmities*. One meaning of the word *help* has a medical connotation, suggesting the way a nurse helps in the healing process. So it is not simply "to take hold of on the other side," which is the literal meaning of the verb, but that the Holy Spirit becomes our partner and helper, who works along with us in a mutual participation, for our healing.

What is our part in the healing of our damaged emotions? The Holy Spirit is, indeed, the divine counselor, the divine psychiatrist, who gets ahold of our problem on the other end. But we're on this end of it. Just what are you and I supposed to do in this healing process?

That is the very purpose of this book and you will find many suggestions as you read further. However, at this point let me suggest the general, biblical principles which must be followed throughout in order for you to find healing for damaged emotions.

1. Face your problem squarely. With rigorous moral honesty, and with God's grace, confront that awful, hidden childhood memory, however deep the feelings within you. Acknowledge it to yourself, and acknowledge it to another human being. Some problems can never be solved until you confess them to others. "Confess your faults one to another, and pray for one another, that you may be healed" (James 5:16). Some people miss deep inner healing because they lack the courage to share deeply with another person.

2. Accept your responsibility in the matter. "But," you say, "I was sinned against. I was a victim. You don't know what happened to me."

True enough. But what about your response? What about the fact that you learned to hate or resent, or to escape into an unreal world?

You may say, "My folks never told me anything about sex, and I grew up and I went out into this evil world, innocent and ignorant, and got into trouble." That's the way it happened the first time. But what about the second time or the third time—whose fault was it then? Life is like a complicated tapestry, woven with a loom and shuttle. Heredity, environment, all the things experienced in childhood, from parents, teachers, playmates, all of life's handicaps— all of these things are on one side of the loom, and they pass the shuttle to you. But remember, you pass the shuttle back through the loom. And this action, together with your responses, weaves the design in the tapestry of your life. You are responsible for your actions. You will never receive healing for your damaged emotions until you stop blaming everyone else and accept your responsibility.

3. Ask yourself if you want to be healed. This is what Jesus asked the sick man who had lain ill for thirty-eight years (John 5:6). Do you really want to be healed, or do you just want to talk about your problem? Do you want to use your problem to get sympathy from others? Do you just want it for a crutch, so that you can walk with a limp?

The lame man said to Jesus, "But, Lord, nobody puts me into the pool. I try, but they all get there ahead of me." He would not look deep within his heart to find out whether he really wanted to be healed.

We live in an age that some call the "goof-off" era, where each person wants to blame someone else instead of facing his own responsibilities. I have been working with college students for many years, and sometimes I wonder what the B.A. degree really means: Bachelor of Arts or Builder of Alibis. Ask yourself: "Do I really want to be healed? Am I willing to face my responsibility in the matter?"

4. *Forgive everyone who is involved in your problem.* Facing responsibility and forgiving people are really two sides of the same coin. The reason some people have never been able to forgive is that if they forgave, the last rug would be pulled out from under them and they would have no one to blame. Facing responsibility and forgiving are almost the same action; in some instances you need to do them simultaneously. Jesus made it very plain that no healing occurs until there is deep forgiveness.

5. *Forgive yourself.* So many Christians say, "Yes, I know that God has forgiven me, but I can never forgive myself." This statement is a contradiction in terms. How can you really believe that God has forgiven you, and then not forgive yourself? When God forgives, He buries your sins in the sea of His forgiveness and His forgetfulness. As Corrie ten Boom said, "He then puts a sign on the bank which says: 'No fishing allowed.'" You have no right to dredge up anything that God has forgiven and forgotten. He has put it behind His back. Through an inscrutable mystery, divine omniscience has somehow forgotten your sins. You can forgive yourself.

6. *Ask the Holy Spirit to show you what your real problem is, and how you need to pray.* Paul said that often we do not know how to pray as we ought (Rom. 8:26). But the Holy Spirit prays in and through us, and makes intercession for us. Sometimes the Holy Spirit uses a temporary assistant in the form of a human counselor, who can help us to perceive what the real problem is. Sometimes the Spirit is able to do this through God's Word or through some incident in life that suddenly makes us aware of our real problem. For it is important that we realize the true problem and know how we should pray. James reminded us that we sometimes do not receive because we pray for the wrong things (James 4:3). It may be essential for you to get help from a counselor or a pastor or a friend; then together with this person, you can ask the Holy Spirit to show you where your real need is.

Do you remember the story of Henry Ford and Charlie Steinmetz? Steinmetz was a dwarf, ugly and deformed, but he had one of the greatest minds in the field of electricity that the world has ever known. Steinmetz built the great generators for Henry Ford in his first plant in Dearborn, Michigan. One day those generators broke down and the plant came to a halt. They brought in ordinary mechanics and helpers who couldn't get the generators going again. They were losing money. Then Ford called Steinmetz. The genius came, seemed to just putter around for a few hours, and then threw the switch that put the great Ford plant back into operation.

A few days later Henry Ford received a bill from Steinmetz for $10,000. Although Ford was a very rich man, he returned the bill with a note, "Charlie, isn't this bill just a little high for a few hours of tinkering around on those motors?"

Steinmetz returned the bill to Ford. This time it read: "For tinkering around on the motors: $10. For knowing where to tinker: $9,990. Total: $10,000." Henry Ford paid the bill.

The Holy Spirit knows where to tinker. We do not know what we ought to be praying for. We often do not receive, because we ask for the wrong things. As you read these chapters, ask the Holy Spirit to show you what you need to know about yourself, and then to guide you in your prayers.

PRAYERFUL REFLECTION

■ Read back through the six principles for healing Dr. Seamands mentions. With which of these principles might you struggle most as you work through this book? Tell God about it. Write a prayer, expressing to Him how you are feeling right now about letting the Holy Spirit "tinker" in your life at an emotional level.

Dear God,

_____

_____

_____

_____

_____

_____

_____

_____

_____

_____

PERSONAL RENEWAL

■ Renew your thoughts and feelings this week by meditating on Romans 8:26-27.

In the same way, the Spirit helps us in our weakness. We do not know what we ought to pray, but the Spirit Himself intercedes for us with groans that words cannot express. And He who searches our hearts knows the mind of the Spirit, because the Spirit intercedes for the saints in accordance with God's will.

Therefore, the kingdom of heaven is like a king who wanted to settle accounts with his servants. As he began the settlement, a man who owed him ten thousand talents was brought to him. Since he was not able to pay, the master ordered that he and his wife and his children and all that he had be sold to repay the debt.

The servant fell on his knees before him. "Be patient with me," he begged, "and I will pay back everything." The servant's master took pity on him, canceled the debt and let him go.

But when that servant went out, he found one of his fellow servants who owed him a hundred denarii. He grabbed him and began to choke him. "Pay back what you owe me!" he demanded.

His fellow servant fell to his knees and begged him, "Be patient with me, and I will pay you back."

But he refused. Instead, he went off and had the man thrown into prison until he could pay the debt. When the other servants saw what had happened, they were greatly distressed and went and told their master everything that had happened.

Then the master called the servant in. "You wicked servant," he said, "I canceled all that debt of yours because you begged me to. Shouldn't you have had mercy on your fellow servant just as I had on you?" In anger his master turned him over to the jailers to be tortured, until he should pay back all he owed.

This is how My Heavenly Father will treat each of you unless you forgive your brother from your heart.

Matthew 18:23-35, NIV

Forgive us our debts, as we forgive our debtors.

Matthew 6:12

Chapter 2
Guilt, Grace, and Debt-Collecting

With the Parable of the Unmerciful Servant, Jesus put into living color and stereophonic sound His teachings about forgiveness. This parable is filled with profound insights about spiritual and emotional healing. We shouldn't be surprised at this. Jesus was the only normal and perfectly sane person who has ever lived. We are told that He knew what was in man, and at the deepest levels. So we should expect His truths, His teachings, to contain the most penetrating psychological truths.

When the king decided to settle his accounts, he found that one servant owed him the fantastic sum of 10 million dollars. Jesus used an impossible sum of money in this parable. The annual taxes from the provinces of Judea, Idumea, Samaria, Galilee, and Perea all put together only amounted to $800,000. But the exaggerated size of the debt is the whole point. A person's debt to God and to others is so great that it can never be paid back, any more than a servant working for a few cents a day could ever save up enough money to repay a debt of 10 million dollars.

The servant fell on his knees and begged for mercy. He was asking for a special kind of mercy, *makrothumason*. Every time this word is used in the New Testament, it means "an extension of time, a delay." "Lord, have patience with me. Please delay and I'll pay you back everything. Give me more time."

We see that the servant's idea of forgiveness was one thing, but the lord's idea was another. The lord in his mercy forgave him all his debts and released him.

But that same servant as he went out saw a fellow servant, a coworker, who owed him a measly twenty bucks. He seized him by the throat and said, "Pay me what you owe me." When the coworker couldn't do it, the servant showed no mercy on him but put him into the debtor's prison until he paid in full.

Then the lord summoned the servant and said, "Look, I forgave you all your debts and now you treat your fellow servant this way." So in anger the lord delivered him to prison until he should pay all.

Now that's bad enough, but Jesus' next statement is the real shocker. "So also My Heavenly Father will do to every one of you if you do not forgive your brother from your heart."

Wait a minute, Jesus. What are you trying to tell us? What kind of picture of the Heavenly Father is this? Is it a mistranslation? No, the inference is clear. To the unforgiven and the unforgiving, God will be like a harsh and stern debt-collector.

Is this an exaggeration, like the inflated sum of money? Or does it refer to the future life, to the punishment of the wicked? It may include those, but we don't have to wait until the next life to see Jesus' words come true. For here and now, the unforgiven and unforgiving person is plagued with guilt and resentment. He lives in a prison house where he finds himself tortured by all manner of inner emotional conflicts.

PERSONAL REFLECTION

■ Are guilt and resentment keeping you emotionally imprisoned today? Complete the following statements, listing everything that comes to mind in response to each statement.

I feel guilty about _____

_____

_____

_____

I feel resentment toward_____for

_____

I feel resentment toward_____for

_____

I feel resentment toward_____for

_____

Other resentments:_____

_____

■ What does being forgiven look like to you? Describe a time when you felt forgiven. For what did you need to be forgiven? How did you go about seeking forgiveness in that situation?

_____

_____

_____

_____

■ Do you see yourself as a forgiving or an unforgiving person? Why? Can you think of a situation in which you found it difficult to forgive another person? Write a brief description of the situation.

_____

_____

_____

_____

_____

Woven into Jesus' parable is a picture of human relationships. The world is made for forgiveness; it is made for grace; it is made for love in all of life. The need for these has been built into the structure of nature, of persons. It is in every cell of our bodies, in every interpersonal relationship. We are made for grace and love and acceptance.

PERSONAL REFLECTION

■ How often we need to remind ourselves of God's grace and love and acceptance. Choose a photograph of yourself you like and glue it in the space provided to remind yourself of God's grace, love, and acceptance.

I AM UNCONDITIONALLY LOVED AND ACCEPTED BY GOD.

One of the biblical descriptions of sin is "violation of God's laws." When we break those laws we are, in a sense, in debt to them. The words *ought* and *owe* come from the same root. To say, "I ought to do this," or "I ought not to do this," is like saying, "I owe it to God," or "I owe it to this person" to do this or not to do this.

What is true about God's laws is also true in the realm of interpersonal relationships. We feel *oughts* and *debts* to one another. When we sin against a person, we often say, "Somehow I feel as if I'm in debt to him," or "I feel as if she owes me an apology." When a person is released from prison, we say he has paid his *debt* to society.

Jesus put this concept at the very heart of the Lord's Prayer when He taught us to pray, "Forgive us our debts as we forgive those who owe us debts." A pastor, counselor, or anyone who works closely with human beings knows that this whole debt system has been built into the human personality in a most incredible fashion. There is a sense of *oughtness*, of *owing* a debt, an automatic mechanism by which the built-in-debt collectors go to work. We seek to atone for those wrongs, to pay the debt we owe, or to collect the debt that someone else owes us. If we feel anger at ourselves, we say, "I must pay in full." Or if we feel anger at someone else, he or she must pay. In this way the whole inexorable process is set in motion as the personality is turned over to the inner tormentors. They are the jailers who work as debt-collectors in this awful prison.

Some of us remember the defensive lineup of the Los Angeles Rams of a few years ago. Half a ton of human flesh simply buried the opposition. They were called the Fearsome Foursome. Jesus is saying that the unforgiven and the unforgiving get turned over to a Fearsome Foursome of *guilt, resentment, striving,* and *anxiety.* These four produce stress, conflict, and all sorts of emotional problems.

THE FEARSOME FOURSOME OF UNFORGIVENESS

YIELDS

STRESS

CONFLICT

EMOTIONAL PROBLEMS

GUILT

RESENT-MENT

STRIV-ING

ANXIETY

Dr. David Belgum, commenting on the claim that up to seventy-five percent of the people in hospitals today with physical illnesses have sicknesses rooted in emotional causes, says that these patients are punishing themselves with their illnesses; and that their physical symptoms and break-downs may be their involuntary confessions of guilt (*Guilt: Where Psychology and Religion Meet,* Prentice-Hall, p. 54).

PERSONAL REFLECTION

■ The doctors of Minirth-Meier Clinic West have defined forgiveness as "the act of setting someone free from an obligation that is the result of a wrong done against you." Forgiveness is NOT excusing or minimizing the wrong that has been done. Rather, it is consciously acknowledging the wrong and purposely choosing to *pardon* the person by whom you've been wronged. Make a list of persons you need to pardon. Briefly describe what it is they have done wrong to you. Then, jot down any barriers you feel are standing in the way of your pardoning them. REMEMBER: Forgiveness is as much for YOUR SAKE as it is for the other person's sake. Pardoning the past frees you to love in the present.

Who? _____

For What? _____

_____

_____

Barriers?_____

_____

Who? _____

For What? _____

_____

_____

Barriers?_____

Who? _____

For What? _____

_____

_____

Barriers?_____

Who ?_____

For What? _____

_____

_____

Barriers?_____

Many years ago I was driven to the conclusion that the two major causes of most emotional problems among evangelical Christians are these: the failure to understand, receive, and live out God's unconditional grace and forgiveness; and the failure to give out that unconditional love, forgiveness, and grace to other people.

1. *Failure to receive forgiveness.* So many of us are like that servant in the parable. Because he misunderstood the offer the lord gave him, he pled for an extension of time. And what happened? The lord in his mercy gave him far more than he asked for, more than he could dream about or pray for; he released him and forgave him all his debts.

But the servant never heard what the lord said to him. He thought that his master had given him what he asked for. And what did he ask for? Patience and extension of time. "Lord, please don't foreclose on my debt. Extend my promissory note a little longer and I assure you I'll pay you everything I owe you." And in his pride and moral stupidity, he thought he could pay back ten million dollars, if he was only given enough time. But the master in his mercy wiped out the whole debt. He didn't extend the note. He tore it up. He canceled it, and *set* the man *free* from his debts, free from the threat of imprisonment.

The poor servant really couldn't believe the wonderful news. He couldn't receive it. He couldn't live it. He couldn't enjoy it. He thought he was still under sentence as a debtor and he'd simply been given more time to work and skimp, and to save and then pay what he owed. Because he didn't realize the debt had been canceled, the hidden tormentors of resentment, guilt, striving, and anxiety went to work in him. Because he thought he still owed, he thought he still had to pay, and also to collect debts from others.

Many of us are like that. We read, we hear, we believe a good theology of grace. But that's not the way we live. We believe grace in our heads but not in our gut level feelings or in our relationships. There's no other word we throw around more piously. We affirm grace in our creeds and sing about it in our hymns. We proclaim it as distinctive of the Christian faith—that we are saved by grace alone through faith. But it's all on a head level. The good news of the Gospel of grace has not penetrated the level of our emotions. It hasn't worked its way into our interpersonal relationships. We rattle off the definition: "Grace is God's undeserved favor." But it's not in our feelings. It's not in our living. We don't go far enough.

Grace is not only God's undeserved mercy and favor. It is also unearned and can never be repaid. The failure to see and know and feel grace drives many Christians to the tragic treadmill of performing, achieving, and striving. They try to get rid of their guilt. They try to atone and pay the debt. They read an extra chapter in the Bible and extend their prayertime for another ten minutes, and then go out and do some guilty witnessing. And what they have is salvation by promissory note.

PERSONAL REFLECTION

■ Think about this: "Your failure to SEE and KNOW and FEEL God's grace in your life will drive you to the tragic treadmill of performing, achieving, and striving." In what ways, if any, is your relationship with Christ based on your performance? Try to identify any DO and/or DON'T DO messages you tell yourself that may be keeping you stuck on the treadmill of performance-based Christianity. *EXAMPLE: "Anger is bad and if I am a good Christian, I will never get angry." "God won't bless my life if I don't give my time and resources to the church." "Admitting a weakness or expressing a need means that I am not trusting God in my life."*

_____

_____

_____

_____

_____

_____

_____

_____

■ According to A.W. Tozer, "What comes into our minds when we think about God is the most important thing about us. For this reason the gravest question before the church is always God Himself, and the most portentous fact about any man is not what he at a given time may say or do, but what he in his deep heart conceives God to be like" (*The Knowledge of the Holy,* Harper & Row, p. 9). Based on your experience with those who have been or are the spiritual authorities in your life, what is your heartfelt concept of God right now?

_____

_____

_____

_____

_____

_____

■ Are you able to accept God's love and grace for you (based solely on who you are to Him), or are you working for His approval (based on what you DO for Him)? Explain.

_____

_____

_____

_____

_____

Many Christians are like the young minister who once came to see me. He was having a lot of problems getting along with other people, especially his wife; she was a very fine person—attractive, warm, affectionate, loving—and totally supported him in his ministry. But he was continually criticizing her, scapegoating her. Everything she did was wrong. He was sarcastic and demanding, and withdrew from her advances, rejected her love and affection. Slowly but surely it began to dawn on him: he was destroying their marriage.

Then he realized that in his weekend pastorate he was hurting people through sermons which were excessively harsh and judgmental. You can do that, you know. He was working out all of his unhappiness on other people.

Finally, in his desperation, he came to see me. At the beginning of our interview, he met trouble like a real man: he blamed it on his wife! But after a while, when he became honest, the painful root of the matter came to light.

While he was in the armed forces in Korea, he had spent two weeks of R and R in Japan. During that leave, walking the streets of Toyko, feeling empty, lonely, and terribly homesick, he fell into temptation and went three or four times to a prostitute.

He had never been able to forgive himself. He had sought God's forgiveness, and with his head, believed he had it. But the guilt still plagued him and he hated himself. Every time he looked in the mirror, he couldn't stand what he was seeing. He had never shared this with anyone and the burden was becoming intolerable.

When he returned home to marry his fiancée, who had faithfully waited for him all those years, his emotional conflicts increased because he still could not accept complete forgiveness. He couldn't forgive himself for what he had done to himself and to her; so he couldn't accept her freely offered affection and love. He felt he had no right to be happy. He said to himself, "I have no right to enjoy my wife. I have no right to enjoy my life. I've got to pay back the debt."

The terrible tormentors were at work within him and he was trying to punish himself, to suffer, to atone for all of his guilt. All those years he lived in a prison house, with the debt-collectors doing their deadly work. As A.W. Tozer put it, the young minister was living in "the perpetual penance of regret."

How beautiful it was to see him receive full, free forgiveness from God, then from his wife, and perhaps best of all, from himself. Sure he was a Christian. He believed and even preached grace, but he had never completely accepted God's forgiveness. He was trying to repay by promissory note. He was doing a self-atonement job, with the guilt disposal unit going inside him.

There is no forgiveness from God unless you freely forgive your brother from your heart. And I wonder if we have been too narrow in thinking that *brother* only applied to someone else. What if *you* are the brother or sister who needs to be forgiven, and you need to forgive *yourself*? Does it not apply to *you* too? The Lord says to forgive your enemies. What if *you* are the worst enemy? Does that exclude *you*? This serviceman-minister had to realize that to forgive the other brother meant to forgive himself also. Anger and resentment against yourself, a refusal to forgive yourself—these are just as damaging when directed at yourself as when they are directed against other people.

PERSONAL
REFLECTION

■ Is there anything you've done for which you have been unable to forgive yourself? Name that failure specifically. Then list all the ways you have tried to dull the pain and memory of that failure by personally trying to atone for your guilt in relation to it.

_____

_____

_____

_____

_____

_____

_____

_____

2. *Failure to give forgiveness.* When we fail to accept and receive God's grace and forgiveness, we also fail to give unconditional love, forgiveness, and grace to other people. And this results in a breakdown in our interpersonal relationships. It results in emotional conflicts between us and other people. The unforgiven are the unforgiving, and the unforgiving complete the vicious circle because they cannot be forgiven.

How tragic is this parable! The servant, not realizing he was completely forgiven, thought he still had to go around collecting money from the servants who owed him, so that he could pay the lord a debt—that had been canceled. He went home, checked his ledger, and said, "I've got to get all this money because I told the master I would pay him back." And what happened? He grabbed hold of the first fellow servant he found, seized him by the throat, and said, "Pay me what you owe me. Give me that twenty bucks."

Think of it. He thought he had at least been given an extension on his promissory note. He wouldn't even give this guy more time, but said, "Pay me right now or I'll throw you in prison." When the poor fellow didn't have the money, he was sent to jail. Not a very healthy way to maintain good interpersonal relationships!

The vicious circle becomes more vicious. The unaccepted are the unaccepting. The unforgiven are the unforgiving. The ungraced are the ungracious. In fact, their behavior is sometimes positively disgraceful. And emotional conflicts and broken relationships are the result.

Think of how you apply this to the significant others in your life: *parents* who hurt you when you were growing up; *brothers and sisters* who failed you when you needed help, who teased you, and put you down; a *friend* who betrayed you; a *sweetheart* who rejected you; your *marriage partner*, who promised to love, honor, comfort, and care for you, but instead has nagged or scapegoated or caused you pain. They all owe you a debt, don't they?

They owe you affection and love, security and affirmation, but since you feel indebted and guilty, resentful, insecure, and anxious, since you see yourself as unforgiven and unacceptable, you in turn become unforgiving and unaccepting. You have not received grace, so how can you give it to others? And as you feel tormented, you hurt others. You've got to collect on the grievances, collect on your hurts. You must make all these people who have hurt you pay the debts they own you. You are a grievance collector.

PERSONAL REFLECTION

■ Have you experienced a breakdown in relationship with any of the following people? (Check ALL that apply to your situation.)

_____Your parents

_____Your grandparents

_____A brother or sister

_____A friend

_____A sweetheart

_____Your marriage partner

_____An employer

_____Others:_____

_____

■ For each of the categories you checked above, write a brief description expressing how that person injured you. Be specific in describing the hurt, using as many *feeling words* as you can to tell why you feel like you do about that person and what happened.

_____

_____

_____

_____

_____

_____

_____

_____

_____

_____

_____

NOTE: *Additional space for journaling is provided on pages 233-237 of this workbook.*

Many married people fail to allow God to do for them what only God can do. Then they ask other human beings, their spouses, to do what they cannot possibly do. If they work at it, men make good husbands, and women make good wives. But they make lousy gods. They're not meant for that. And all those wonderful promises that people make on their wedding day—"I promise to love, care for you, cherish you, through all the circumstances and vicissitudes of life"—these are possible only when a heart is secure in God's love, grace, and care. Only a forgiven and graced soul can keep such promises. What the person often really means when he says those beautiful words is, "I have a lot of terrific inner needs and inner emptiness and debts to pay and I'm going to give you a marvelous opportunity to fill my Grand Canyon and take care of me. Aren't I wonderful?"

Psychologist Larry Crabb compares this behavior to a tick on a dog. The tick isn't really interested in a good life for the dog; he's simply taking all the time. You see, the tragedy with some marriages is that both partners are takers, and the marriage is like two ticks and no dog! Two collectors and nothing to collect.

Many years ago a couple came to see me. They'd been married fifteen years. Fifteen years of marital Ping-Pong. Every time he pinged, she ponged, or vice versa. Offensive and defensive play alternated. As we slowly and painfully counseled together, we first had to remove some theological wrappings to uncover the terrible disappointment, hurt, and real resentment they felt against one another. She had married *him* for his spiritual leadership—he had been a VIP on campus. He seemed disciplined, firm, and hardworking—a young man who would really go places for the Lord.

You can imagine her shock when he turned out to be indecisive, and undisciplined, lazy and procrastinating. In her anger she, like the servant of old, was seizing him by the throat and saying, "You cheated me. You owe me all those expectations I had when I married you." She saw him as a person in debt to her. With her nagging words she had spent fifteen years saying, "Pay me what you owe me, old man."

But, you see, he had married *her* for her good looks and her neatness and orderliness. You can imagine his terrible disappointment when he discovered she was sloppy about the housework, careless about her hair and dress and appearance. He felt she had cheated him. "You owe me these things because this is the promise you gave me in courtship; this is who I thought you were. You made me these promises." And so he was seizing her by the throat, and with his sarcasm and cutting remarks, was saying, "Pay me what you owe me. You didn't come through on your promissory note."

Each one had been waiting fifteen years for the other one to change. Oh, the tragedy of interpersonal relationships among professing Christians. We are debt-collectors. We are grievance collectors. Why? Because we don't realize our debt has been fully canceled, that it's over. Although God has torn up the note at Calvary, we're still trying so hard to pay.

After I preached about debt-collecting at a counseling conference, I was going up the aisle when a mother grabbed ahold of me. She said, "I never realized it. That's what I've been doing to my kids for the last eighteen years—collecting debts, asking them to pay me what they owed me, instead of giving them unconditional love." And what a lot of hangups it caused.

PERSONAL REFLECTION

■ Is there someone you need to forgive, including yourself? Take these three tests to find out.

1. THE RESENTMENT TEST. *Is there someone you resent, someone you've never let off the hook?* A parent, brother, sister, sweetheart, marriage partner, friend, coworker, someone who wronged you in childhood, some teacher in grade school, or someone who misused you sexually as you grew up? Do a personal resentment inventory in the space provided below, listing the name of anyone you harbor resentment toward at this moment (from the distant past to the immediate present). Before you begin writing, ask God to bring to your mind the name of every person you need to include in this list. *NOTE: This list may include the names of individuals you noted in the Personal Reflection section completed earlier in this chapter.*

_____

_____

_____

2. THE RESPONSIBILITY TEST. *Do you take responsibility for your own faults and failures, or do you blame other people for what happens? (Example of blaming: "Don't worry, David. That wasn't your fault. You would have been OK if only. . . .")* This test is a little trickier. It's easy to pass the buck when we fail or blow it and let someone else become the responsible party. As we find healing and recovery from damaged emotions we learn to extend forgivenss to others and assume responsibility for ourselves. Have you ever *flunked* the Responsibility Test? Cite a time when you blamed someone else for a failure that was really your own fault. What was the end result? Now give an example when you owned up to your own failure and *passed* the Responsibility Test with flying colors.

_____

_____

_____

_____

_____

3. THE REMINDER & REACTION TEST. *Do you find yourself reacting against a person because he or she reminds you of someone else?* This test is actually very subtle. For instance, maybe you don't like the way your husband disciplines your children because he reminds you of your father who overdid it. So that causes a clash. Or you don't like your neighbor, or you respond to a coworker with a bit of anger, a bit of resentment. Why? Because you have never really forgiven someone else. And your reaction to reminders of that unforgiven person from the past triggers resentment against this person. Can you think of anyone with whom you seem to clash or have frequent run-ins? List below the names of any individuals who come to mind. Then try to identify the "person from your past" who continues to haunt you through that person.

_____

_____

_____

_____

_____

_____

_____

_____

There is a scriptural way to deal with all these hurts from our past. God's way goes far beyond forgiving and surrendering resentment. God takes sins, failures, and hurts that happened earlier in your life and wraps His loving purposes around them to change them.

The greatest illustration of this is the cross. There God took what, from a human standpoint, was the worst injustice and the deepest tragedy that ever happened and turned it into the most sublime gift man has ever known: the gift of salvation.

We see a human illustration of this in the life of Joseph who had been so brutally wronged by his older brothers. When his brothers later groveled before Joseph the ruler, there was no debt-collecting on his part; no leaning heavily on them. He wasn't concerned about collecting the debt. Instead, because he knew they were going to have a hard time forgiving themselves, he said, "Have no fear; for am I in God's place. True enough, you planned evil against me, but God planned it for good, to bring about what today is fact, the keeping alive of much people" (Gen. 50:19-20, BERK).

Are you part of a debt-free community of Christians? Is your marriage free of debt-collecting? Your family? Every church should be a debt-free society, where we love each other because we are loved. Where we accept because we are accepted. Where we grace one another and are gracious because we have been graced, because we know the joy of having seen the Master tear up the charge card that we have spent beyond paying. It's been canceled. He's torn it up. He doesn't add something more to it and say, "Well, I'll give you a little more time to repay."

And so because He has set us free, we can set others free and thereby set in motion grace and love. The Apostle Paul summed it up in nine words: "Owe no man anything, but to love one another" (Rom. 13:8).

In Jesus' words, "Freely you have received, freely give," the root word for *gift* is used four times, so that it literally says, "Giftwise you have been given, giftwise give!" (Matt. 10:8)

PRAYERFUL REFLECTION

■ Are you ready to deal honestly with the hurts from your past? Do you really want to be set free from the "fearsome foursome of unforgiveness"—resentment, guilt, striving, and anxiety? Is there anything that keeps you from extending forgiveness to people who have hurt you? Are you willing to forgive yourself for past failures in your life? Are you ready to seek forgiveness from any persons you have harmed? Answer these questions in the form of a prayer to God. Tell Him just how you feel about the things you've discovered about yourself as you've worked the material in this chapter. Ask Him to help you take the next step in your journey of healing, whatever that might be. Thank Him for canceling your debt in full and setting you free.

Lord Jesus,

_____

_____

_____

_____

_____

PERSONAL RENEWAL

■ Renew your thoughts and feelings this week by meditating on Psalm 86:5 and Psalm 103:2-4. *NOTE: The personal pronouns my/me have been added in brackets for emphasis.*

> *You are forgiving and good, O Lord, abounding in love to all who call to you. . . . Praise the Lord, O my soul, and forget not all His benefits—who forgives all [my] sins and heals all [my] diseases, who redeems [my] life from the pit and crowns [me] with love and compassion.*

Seeing then that we have a great High Priest, that is passed into the heavens, Jesus the Son of God, let us hold fast our profession. For we have not an High Priest which cannot be touched with the feeling of our infirmities; but was in all points tempted like as we are, yet without sin. Let us therefore come boldly unto the throne of grace, that we may obtain mercy, and find grace to help in time of need. . . .

In the days of His flesh, when He had offered up prayers and supplications with strong crying and tears unto Him that was able to save Him from death, and was heard in that He feared; though He were a Son, yet learned He obedience by the things which He suffered; and being made perfect, He became the author of eternal salvation unto all them that obey Him.

Hebrews 4:14-16; 5:7-9

Chapter 3
The Wounded Healer

If we were to rephrase Hebrews 4:15 as a positive statement, it would read: "For we have a High Priest who is touched with the feeling of our infirmities." In the Old Testament, the word *infirmity* is connected with the sacrifices offered by the priests. An infirmity was primarily a physical spot, a blemish. It was a defect or a deformity either in a man or in an animal. If a man had an infirmity, even though he was a member of the priestly family of Aaron, he could not function as a priest. His infirmity disqualified him from entering the presence of the holiness of God (Lev. 21:16-24). In the same way, offerings and sacrifices had to be "without spot or blemish." Scores of references in the Book of Leviticus make plain that no infirm animal could be offered to God. Both the offering and the offerer had to be free from infirmities.

In the New Testament we begin to see a figurative use of the word *infirmity*. It is a metaphor, a figure of speech. The common New Testament word for *infirmity* is the negative form of *sthenos* which means "strength." Now, when you put the letter *a* in front of something, that negates it. A *theist* is one who believes in God; you put an *a* in front of the word and it becomes *atheist*, one who does not believe in God. If you put an *a* in front of *sthenos*, which means "strength," you get the root word for infirmity, *astheneia*, "a want of strength, a lack of strength, a weakness, an infirmity, a crippling."

The word is hardly ever used in a purely physical sense in the New Testament. Rather, it refers to mental, moral, and emotional weakness, to lack of strength. Infirmities in themselves are not sins, but they do undermine our resistance to temptation. In the New

Testament, infirmities are qualities in human nature which may predispose or incline us to sin, sometimes without any conscious choice on our part.

PERSONAL REFLECTION

■ Infirmities are crippling weaknesses that sabotage our happiness and relationships and keep us from taking responsibility for our own lives. These weaknesses may be mental, moral, or emotional and will be worked out in our lives through our attitudes, feelings, and behaviors. Oftentimes we think, feel, and do these things without any conscious choice on our part. *EXAMPLES:* perfectionism—*the compulsive drive to do things perfectly*; indecisiveness—*having a difficult time making decisions*; blaming—*inability to take responsibility for your own thoughts or actions*. What crippling weaknesses are sabotaging your happiness and relationships at present? Make a list of "infirmities" in your life of which you are aware.

_____

_____

_____

_____

_____

The Book of Hebrews is more like the Book of Leviticus than any other book in the New Testament, and shows that the sacrificial system outlined in Leviticus finds its fulfillment in Jesus Christ, our High Priest. This fulfillment also applies to the matter of infirmities in the priests. The Old Testament priest had infirmities because he shared in the common lot of all human beings. Therefore, when he made his sacrifices, he was also sacrificing for himself to cover all his imperfection, as well as presenting an offering for his people. However, because he had infirmities, he could understand the infirmities of his people and deal more gently with them. He could be more understanding as a priest. For he too was subjected to the inner infirmities which predispose all of us to temptation and sin.

The writer to the Hebrews applied this picture to our great High Priest and Mediator, our Lord Jesus Christ. Because He never sinned, because He never yielded to the temptations unlike the Old Testament priest, He never had to make a sacrifice on His own behalf. But since He was tempted, since He was tested at every point as we are, we have a great High Priest who understands *the feeling of our infirmities.*

If He merely understood the *fact* of our infirmities, that would be good enough. But I've got better news for you. He even understands the *feeling* of our infirmities—not just the cripplings, not just the weakness, not just the emotional hangups and the inner conflicts, but the pain that comes from them. He understand the frustration, the anxiety, the depression, the hurts, the feelings of abandonment and loneliness and isolation and rejection. He who is touched with the feeling of our infirmities experiences the whole ghastly gamut of emotions which goes along with our weakness and our cripplings.

And what's the proof of this? To what does the writer to the Hebrews turn to show that Jesus understands how we feel as a result of our infirmities? "In the days of His flesh," while Jesus was human, He "offered up prayers and supplications" (Heb. 5:7). In a beautiful, soft quiet time? Oh, no. He "offered up prayers and supplications with strong crying and tears unto Him that was able to save Him from death, and was heard in that He feared. Though He were a Son, yet learned He obedience by the things which He suffered" (Heb. 5:7-8).

This points to Gethsemane, to the passion and suffering, to the cross of our Lord, as if to say, "There, He has experienced it all. He knows what it is to cry out with tears. He knows what it is to pray to God with loud sobs. He wrestled with feelings that nearly tore Him to pieces. He knows. He's been through it, and can feel with you. He hurts along with you."

PERSONAL REFLECTION

■ Think of a time when you wrestled with feelings (anger, sadness, anxiety, loneliness) that nearly tore you to pieces. Describe it below.

_____

_____

_____

_____

_____

■ Can you recall any instances in your life when someone provided an understanding ear and unusual empathy in relation to a painful situation you were going through at that point in time? How did it make you feel knowing that person understood and cared?

_____

_____

_____

_____

_____

_____

Of all the words for the Incarnation, the greatest title is *Emmanuel,* "God with us." God is in it with us. Better still, God having gone through it Himself knows how to be in it and feel it with us. That is why we can come boldly; we can draw near with confidence. God doesn't say, "You can come guiltily," or "You can come shamefacedly." You never need to feel, *There's something wrong with me because I'm feeling depressed; I must not be spiritual.* These are cruelties we Christians often inflict on one another, and they are not biblical.

We are not coming into the presence of a neurotic parent who has to hear only good things from his children. We're not coming into the presence of a father who says, "Shhh, don't feel that way; that's wrong. Don't cry. If you keep crying I'll really give you something to cry about."

We are coming to a Heavenly Father who understands our feelings and invites us to share them with Him. So we can draw near with confidence unto the throne of grace knowing that we will obtain mercy and find grace in our time of need. We can come when we need forgiveness and when we feel guilty for our sins. And we can also come when we are being racked and tormented by the feelings of our infirmities.

PERSONAL REFLECTION

■ Is there anything you want to express right now to Emmanuel— "God who is with us in it"? Is there guilt or loneliness or sadness? Fear, frustration, or helplessness? Share those feelings with God in the form of a written prayer, knowing this—you can draw near to Him with confidence. God knows your place of pain and understands it.

_____

_____

_____

_____

_____

_____

_____

To understand what it cost the Savior to be our Healer, we need to walk with Him through His passion and suffering, as shown in the Gospels, in the Psalms, and in the Book of Isaiah.

Come with me now into the Garden of Gethsemane. Discover what it cost our Savior to be Emmanuel, God with us. Listen to His prayers. Can you hear them, as if for the first time? He "began to be sorrowful and very heavy. Then saith He unto them, 'My soul is exceeding sorrowful, even unto death'" (Matt. 26:37-38).

Wait a minute, Jesus. What did You say? "My soul is exceeding _sorrowful, even unto death_"? Do You mean to say that You experienced such feelings, such emotions and pain in that wretched hour, that You even wanted to die? Do You mean to say, Lord, You understand when I am so depressed that I no longer want to live?

PERSONAL REFLECTION

■ Look up Matthew 26:36-39 and read it before answering the following question: Have you ever felt the way Jesus did in these verses? Describe your experience

_____

_____

_____

_____

_____

Look at Psalm 22, one of the so-called Psalms of Dereliction: "I am poured out like water, and all my bones are out of joint; my heart is like wax; it is melted. . . . My strength is dried up like a potsherd [clay in the baking]; and my tongue cleaveth to my jaws; and Thou hast brought me into the dust of death" (vv. 14-15).

Psalm 69 is another: "Save me, O God; for the waters are come in unto my soul" (v. 1). "I am come into deep waters, where the floods overflow me" (v. 2). "I am weary of my crying" (v. 3). "Reproach hath broken my heart; and I am full of heaviness: and I looked for some to take pity, but there was none; and for comforters, but I found none" (v. 20).

"Peter, what, could ye not watch with Me for one hour?" (Matt. 26:40) Three times He implored His friends, but to no avail. Finally, "all the disciples forsook Him, and fled" (Matt. 26:56).

If you have battled terrible loneliness, or pathological emptiness, if you have experienced the blackest bouts of depression, you know that when you are in the pits, the hardest thing to do is to pray, because you do not feel God's presence. I want to assure you that He knows, He understands, He feels your infirmity. He shares all your feelings because Has been through them.

Now follow Jesus into the trial, where He listened to false testimony. Have you ever been falsely accused? Do you know the hurt of that? "They spit in His face and buffeted Him; and others smote Him" (Matt. 26:67). "They mocked Him. . . . they struck Him on the face" (Luke 22:63).

So often when I counsel people who are filled with deep hurt, rage, or pain, they will look at me like the great stone face, without even a flicker of emotion. But when I probe more deeply, asking, "Tell me, what's the worst picture in all of your memory? The ones that come most often to bring you pain?" a change comes about. In the beginning only a trace, then the eyes start to fill with tears; soon the overflow comes down the cheeks, and before long, even strong, strapping men are shaking with pain and anger.

"Oh, I know what it is. I remember. It was when Dad would lash out and hit me on the head. It was when Mother would slap me." Nothing is more destructive to a human personality than a slap in the face. It is so humiliating, so demeaning, so deeply dehumanizing. It destroys something very basic to our personhood.

But our wounded Healer understands. He knows what it is to be struck on the head, to be slapped in the face. He is touched with the feelings, the feelings that arise in you from that hurt. He feels the problems that touch you. He wants to heal. He wants you to know that He is not angry with you about your feelings. He understands.

PERSONAL REFLECTION

■ Read Matthew 26:59-68 and 27:27-31. In what ways do you identify with the pain Jesus experienced in these verses? What hurtful memories bring you a similar kind of emotional pain? Describe them.

_____

_____

_____

_____

_____

_____

_____

Let us go even farther until we come to the cross itself. They derided Jesus, wagging their heads and saying, "If Thou be the Son of God, come down from the cross" (Matt. 27:40). They mocked Him, railed Him, scoffed at Him. _Deriding, wagging their heads, mocking, railing, scoffing_—these words bring to mind the growing pains and humiliating hurts of the teen years. One man believes high school is often such a traumatic experience that he's written a book called _Is There Life after High School?_

I am amazed at the painful sights and sounds grownups share with me from their adolescent memories. The sounds that so often come to people's memories are those of derision, like _"Na-na-na-na-na-na."_ Or names like "Smarty," "Fatty," "Clumsy," "Pimple-face," and "Acne." Or was it being reminded of those big horn-rimmed glasses, or those ugly braces for buck teeth? You fill it in. The cruelty of children to one another is a part of life.

Jesus knows how you feel when you are rejected by a friend, cast off by a lover, made fun of by the gang. In the words of Isaiah, "He hath no beauty that we should desire Him. He is despised and rejected of men; a Man of sorrows, and acquainted with grief: and we hid as it were our faces from Him, He was despised, and we esteemed Him not" (Isa. 53:2-3).

Yes, He was a Man or sorrows and acquainted with grief. If you are grieving, He can feel it with you. For the lonely one—the widow or widower, the divorcee—He understands what it is to be alone, to feel that a part of yourself has been literally torn away.

Studies show that the two greatest stress-producing factors to body, mind, and emotions are the death of a spouse and divorce. In some ways, divorce can be worse. The death of a spouse, though painful, can be a clean wound. Divorce often leaves a dirty, infected wound, throbbing with pain. Jesus understand when a single parent is trying to be husband and wife, mother and father, all in one.

PERSONAL REFLECTION

■ Reflect for a moment on the prophetic words of Isaiah concerning Jesus, "He is despised and rejected of men; a Man of sorrows, and acquainted with grief." In what ways are YOU "acquainted with grief"? What difference do these prophetic words about Christ make when it comes to accepting the painful losses of your life?

_____

_____

_____

_____

_____

_____

But does He know the worst feeling of all our infirmities—when we can't even pray? When we feel abandoned and forsaken by God Himself? The Apostles' Creed says, "He descended into hell." When Christ was hanging on the cross, the very heavens became brassy, not brotherly. They became frighteningly deaf as He was cut off from the land of the living. He cried for help in His final anguish but there was no answer. "My God, My God, why hast Thou forsaken Me? Why art Thou so far off from helping Me, and from the words of My roaring? O My God, I cry in the daytime, but Thou hearest not" (Ps. 22:1-2). God understands the cry of dereliction. He knows the feelings of our infirmities.

To say, as do the ancient creeds, that Christ descended into hell, means that Jesus Christ has entered into every one of the fears, terrors, and anxious feelings that you and I can experience at our lowest moments of rejection, forsakenness, and depression. It means there is not a single feeling that we cannot bring to Him.

We do not need to come guiltily, or shamefacedly. We are to approach boldly, with confidence, knowing He not only feels with us, but wants to heal us. And He has not left us alone, for the Holy Spirit helps us with our infirmities (Rom. 8:26). The human experience of Jesus Christ is now with us in the presence of the Holy Spirit who will aid us with our infirmities, in a mutual participation for their healing.

PERSONAL REFLECTION

■ Do you believe in your heart of hearts that there is not a single feeling you cannot bring to God? Do a feelings inventory. Begin with any feelings you are struggling with at present and work your way back as far as you can to the painful feelings of your past. The sentence completions below will help you get started. *Additional space is provided in the back of this workbook if more journaling space is needed.*

Lord Jesus,

Do You really understand how I felt when_____

_____

Do You understand how I felt when _____

_____

Or how I felt when _____

_____

Or how I felt when _____

_____

Young, beautiful, vivacious, athletic Joni Eareckson struck a rock one day when she dived into a lake. Paralysis resulted and she is now a quadraplegic. She paints picture with a brush in her teeth. Her witness has become worldwide through her books and the movie of her life.

Joni realized how really helpless she was one desperate night when she begged a friend to give her some pills so she could die. When her friend refused, she thought, *I can't even die on my own!* At first life was hell for Joni. Pain, rage, bitterness, and emotional pain shook her spirit. Although she couldn't really feel physical pain, piercing sensations racked her nerves and ran through her body. This went on for three years.

Then one night a dramatic change began in Joni that now makes her the beautiful, radiant Christian she is. Her best friend, Cindy, was at her bedside searching desperately for some way to encourage her. It must have come from the Holy Spirit, for she suddenly blurted it out, "Joni, Jesus knows how you feel. You're not the only one who's been paralyzed. He was paralyzed too."

Joni glared at her. "Cindy, what are you talking about?"

"It's true. It's true, Joni. Remember, He was nailed to the cross. His back was raw from beatings like your back sometimes gets raw. Oh, He must have longed to move. To change His position, to redistribute His weight somehow, but He couldn't move. Joni, He knows how you feel."

That was the beginning, as Cindy's words gripped Joni. She had never thought of it before. God's Son had felt the piercing sensations that racked her body. God's Son knew the helplessness she suffered.

Joni later said, "God became incredibly close to me. I had seen what a difference the love shown me by friends and family had made. I began to realize that God also loved me" *(Where Is God When It Hurts?* Phillip Yancey, Zondervan, pp. 118–119).

As Christians we often thank God that Jesus bore our sins in His body on the tree. We need to remember something else. In His full identification with our humanity, and especially on that cross, He took unto Himself the entire range of our feelings. And He bore the feeling of our infirmities, that we would not have to bear them alone.

Most of us are familiar with the words of the traditional folk spiritual, "Lonesome Valley."

> Jesus walked this lonesome valley,
> He had to walk it by Himself;
> O nobody else could walk it for Him,
> He had to walk it by Himself.
>
> You must go and stand your trial,
> You have to stand it by yourself;
> O nobody else can stand it for you,
> You have to stand it by yourself.

But I was delighted that recently Erna Moorman added another stanza which has brought the song much more in line with the message of the Scriptures.

> As we walk our lonesome valley,
> We do not walk it by ourselves;
> For God sent His Son to walk it with us,
> We do not walk it by ourselves.
> *(Hymns for the Family of God,* Paragon Associates, p. 217).

"We have no superhuman High Priest to whom our weaknesses are unintelligible—He Himself has shared fully in all our experience" (Heb. 4:15, PH). It is this assurance which gives us the grounds for our hope and our healing. The fact that God not only knows and cares, *but fully understands* is the most therapeutic factor in the healing of our damaged emotions.

PRAYERFUL REFLECTION

■ How does it make you feel to know that Jesus (who is God . . . the same God who made you) has shared fully in all of your experience? Write a prayer, letting God know how you feel about Him being YOUR "wounded Healer."

Dear God,

_____

_____

_____

_____

_____

_____

PERSONAL RENEWAL

■ Renew your thoughts and feelings this week by meditating on Isaiah 53:2-5. These words were spoken by the Prophet Isaiah approximately 700 years before the birth of Christ and foretold what Christ would suffer during his brief stay in our world.

> *He grew up before Him like a tender shoot, and like a root out of dry ground. He had no beauty or majesty to attract us to Him, nothing in His appearance that we should desire Him. He was despised and rejected by men, a man of sorrows, and familiar with suffering. Like one from whom men hide their faces He was despised, and we esteemed Him not. Surely He took up our infirmities and carried our sorrows, yet we considered Him stricken by God, smitten by Him, and afflicted. But He was pierced for our transgressions, He was crushed for our iniquities; the punishment that brought us peace was upon Him, and by His wounds we are healed.*

Finally, my brethren, be strong in the Lord, and in the power of His might. Put on the whole armor of God, that ye may be able to stand against the wiles of the devil. For we wrestle not against flesh and blood, but against principalities, against powers, against the rulers of the darkness of this world, against spiritual wickedness in high places. . . . Praying always with all prayer and supplication in the Spirit, and watching thereunto with all perseverance.

Ephesians 6:10-12, 18

Lest Satan should get an advantage of us; for we are not ignorant of his devices.

2 Corinthians 2:11

Chapter 4
Satan's Deadliest Weapon

The biblical picture of Satan is quite different from the popular one. In the Bible he is not the comical creature of the cartoons, with horns, tail, and pitchfork, and ludicrously dressed in long red underwear. Rather, Satan is an adversary, who is clever, wily, and dangerous (1 Peter 5:8).

Because he is of the spirit world, Satan knows your weaknesses; he understands your infirmities and uses them to great advantage against you. The Bible doesn't speak as much of the power of Satan as of his extreme *subtlety, trickery,* and *deceptiveness.* He uses clever wiles and devices, stratagems, and designs. He knows how to exploit your weaknesses in the direction of discouragement, disappointment, failure, and abdication of the Christian life. He is spoken of as a roaring lion, prowling about trying to find somebody to devour (1 Peter 5:8). Paul wrote of the evil powers of darkness against which we fight (Eph. 6:12). And it is in the dark that we are easily attacked or deceived.

Some of the most powerful weapons in Satan's arsenal are psychological. Fear is one of these. Doubt is another. Anger, hostility, worry, and of course, guilt. Long-standing guilt is hard to shake off; it seems to hang on even after a Christian claims forgiveness and accepts pardoning grace.

PERSONAL
REFLECTION

■ Of the seven weapons listed on the next page, which ones has Satan used in your life to cause you to feel defeated? Give one or two examples which illustrate how fear, doubt, anger, hostility, worry, guilt, or low self-esteem have struck you down.

_____

_____

_____

_____

_____

_____

_____

SEVEN DEADLY PSYCHOLOGICAL WEAPONS OF SATAN

An uneasy sense of self-condemnation hangs over many Christians like a Los Angeles smog. They find themselves defeated by the most powerful psychological weapon that Satan uses against Christians. This weapon has the effectiveness of a deadly missile. Its name? Low self-esteem.

Satan's greatest psychological weapon is a gut-level feeling of inferiority, inadequacy, and low self-worth. This feeling shackles many Christians, in spite of wonderful spiritual experiences, in spite of their faith and knowledge of God's Word. Although they understand their position as sons and daughters of God, they are tied up in knots, bound by a terrible feeling of inferiority, and chained to a deep sense of worthlessness.

There are four ways that Satan uses this deadliest of all of his emotional and psychological weapons, to bring defeat and failure into your life.

1. Low self-esteem paralyzes your potential. In the places I have ministered, I have seen the awful impact of the feeling of inferiority. I have witnessed the tragic loss in human potential, the watered-down living, the wasted gifts, the leakage of a veritable gold mine of human power and possibility. And inwardly I have wept.

Do you know that God also weeps over it? He is not so much angry as He is grieved. He weeps over the paralysis of your potential through low self-esteem. The cost is so great, for it seems all of us have to struggle against this. Very few people have fully overcome the haunting self-doubts, the dragging disappointments about who they are, and what they can be. Low self-esteem begins even in the crib, follows to kindergarten, and worsens during the teen years. In adult life, it seems to settle in like a great fog that covers many people day by day. Sometimes it lifts a little but always returns, trying to engulf, to drown.

Unfortunately, this is a plague among Christians. In a tape entitled, "Satan's Psychological Warfare," Christian psychologist James Dobson tells about a poll he took among a large group of women. Most of them were married, in excellent health, and happy. According to their own statements, they had happy children and financial security. On the test Dr. Dobson listed ten sources of depression. He asked the women to number them in the order of how the ten affected their lives. This is the list he gave them:

Ten Sources of Depression Among Women

_____Absence of romantic love in your marriage

_____In-law conflicts

_____Low self-esteem

_____Problems with children

_____Financial difficulties

_____Loneliness, isolation, boredom

_____Sexual problems in marriage

_____Health problems

_____Fatigue and time pressure

_____Aging

How would you rank these ten sources of depression? Take a few minutes right now to number the preceding list in the order of how they affect YOUR life.

The women Dr. Dobson interviewed rated these by the amount of depression each produced. What came out way ahead of all the others? Low self-esteem. Fifty percent of these Christian women rated it first; eighty percent of them rated it in the top two or three. Can you see the wasted emotional and spiritual potential? These women were battling depression which came chiefly from the downward pull of feelings of low self-worth.

Jesus told a parable about the talents. The man with the one talent was immobilized by fear and feelings of inadequacy. Because he was so afraid of failure he didn't invest his talent, but buried it in the ground and tried to play it safe. His life was a frozen asset—frozen by fear of rejection by the master, fear of failure, fear of comparison to the other two who were making their investments, fear of taking a risk. He did exactly what a lot of people with low self-esteem do—nothing. And that's exactly what Satan wants for you as a Christian—that you will be so tied up that you are tied down, frozen, paralyzed, settling into a job and a life far below your potential.

PERSONAL REFLECTION

■ How's your self-esteem? Too low? Too high? Appropriate? In her workbook entitled, *Breaking Free*, Pia Mellody states that *"Healthy self-esteem is the internal experience of your own value, or preciousness. It is generated within yourself, rather than coming to you from outside through the positive regard of other people, accomplishments, or possessions. When you experience healthy self-esteem, you know that no matter what mistakes you make or how you look or what your grades were in school or what other people say, you are worthwhile, lovable, and adequate. When you cannot experience healthy self-esteem, you experience esteem in one of two inappropriate ways. At one end of the spectrum is the experience of low or no self-esteem. At the other end is the experience of arrogance and grandiosity, of being better than others"* (*Breaking Free*, Harper & Row, 1989, pp. 29–30). How would you rate your own level of self-esteem?

Describe you as you see yourself today.

_____

_____

_____

_____

_____

_____

■ Describe situations that trigger your sense of being of less value than other people and the thinking that accompanies those feelings of inferiority. *Example: When I see another woman whose beauty I perceive as being greater than mine, I regard myself as ugly and therefore of less value.*

_____

_____

_____

_____

_____

_____

2. *Low self-esteem destroys your dreams.* You've probably heard the old definition, "Neurotics are people who build castles in the air; psychotics are those who move into them; and psychiatrists are the ones who collect the rent!"

However, I am talking about daydreams or unrealistic fantasies. We can't live *in* our dreams, we can't live *on* our dreams, but we do live *by* our dreams. One of the characteristics of Pentecost, as prophesied by Joel and fulfilled in the Book of Acts, was that when the Holy Spirit was poured out, the young would see visions and the old would dream dreams (Acts 2:17). The Holy Spirit helps us to dream bold dreams, to see visions of what God wants to do for us and in us, and especially through us.

PERSONAL REFLECTION

■ Take a minute to get centered on God. Ask His Spirit to help you dream a bold dream of what God wants to do for you, *in* you and *through* you. Write down whatever comes to your mind at this point.

_____

_____

_____

_____

_____

_____

"Where there is no vision, the people perish" (Prov. 29:18). Yes, and with the wrong kind of vision about yourself, with a low-esteeming picture of yourself as inferior and unable, you will surely self-destruct. Your dreams will be destroyed and God's great plan for your life will not be fulfilled.

The greatest illustration of this is in the Old Testament, in the Book of Numbers, chapters 13 and 14. God had a vision for His people, a bold, beautiful dream. He implanted into their hearts and minds the picture of a Promised Land, flowing with milk and honey, a land which they would possess.

God brought them up to the edge of the Promised Land, to the bold plan He had for them. Moses got his orders from the Lord and then sent a military reconnoitering party into the land to look it over. That's the first historical mention of the CIA—the Canaan Information Agency. Moses sent the cream of the crop, the best man from each tribe. And he fully expected that the realities of Canaan would confirm God's dreams and God's promise. And in a sense they did, for all of the scouts agreed: "It's a fantastic land. Look at the fruit—we never saw grapes and pomegranates like that. And the honey—it is the sweetest you have ever tasted!" (See Num. 13:23.)

"But the people are giants of incredible strength. And the cities are not really cities; they're forts. And those descendants of Anak, the

Nephilim—why in their sight we were as grasshoppers." (See Num. 13:31-33.)

Now, you can't have a much lower self-concept than to see yourself as a grasshopper. The envoys began to weep and to be filled with fear. Only Caleb and Joshua had a different story. Oh, they agreed on all the facts. Their *observations* were the same; but because their *perceptions* were different, their *conclusions* were different. Why? Because Caleb was a man of a different spirit (Num. 14:24). There's your answer. Caleb had no worm theology. He and Joshua had no grasshopper esteem of themselves. They said, "Of course the people are big, but don't fear them. The Lord is with us."

I like the Hebrew slang Caleb and Joshua used. "They are as bread for us. We don't care how big they are; we can eat them up just like bread, and we can do this because it is God's will for us. It is God's dream, and He delights to do it in us and through us. He'll give us our dream and give us our land." (See Num. 14:8-10.)

God's great dream, the whole purpose for which He had saved and delivered them from Egypt's slavery was detoured and delayed for forty wretched years in the wilderness. God's dream wasn't a neurotic air castle; it was reality—fruit and honey, land and cities—everything God wanted to give them, all within their reach. The *dream* was ready and *God* was ready but the people weren't because of their low self-esteem. "We are grasshoppers." They forgot they were the children of God. They forgot *who* they were and *what* they were.

How we need this message today. We wrap a lot of fears in morbidly sanctified self-belittling. We piously cover this self-despising and call it consecration and self-crucifixion. It's time we have some bold dreams. It's time we get into the world with our witness, in a far greater way. What holds us back? Fear of criticism, fear of taking a risk, fear of tradition, fear of constituency. In our low self-esteem, we destroy God's dream for us as a community of believers—we who are His very own body.

What happened to your dream? Where is the vision God put before you? What wrecked it? Your sins and transgressions and bad habits? I doubt it. Probably your dream has been delayed or destroyed because Satan tricked you into thinking of yourself as a grasshopper or a worm. And as a result, you never have realized your full potential as a son or daughter of God. You've filled up with fears and doubts, inferiority, and inadequacy.

How far do you think William Carey, the first great Protestant missionary to India, would have gotten without a dream? He expressed it this way: "Expect great things from God, attempt great things for God." That is the kind of divine dream that is destroyed by low self-esteem. Lack of faith in God is often fed by underestimating what He wants to do through you.

PERSONAL REFLECTION

■ What has held you back from pursuing your dreams in the past? What might keep you from seeing the bold dream you described in the previous question fulfilled in your lifetime? What will keep you pressing forward to see your bold dream ultimately fulfilled?

_____

_____

_____

_____

_____

REMEMBER WILLIAM CAREY'S MOTTO: "Expect great things from God, attempt great things for God."

3. *Low self-esteem ruins your relationships.* Think about your relationship with God Himself. It follows quite naturally that if you consider yourself inferior or worthless, you will think that God really must not love and care for you. Such thinking often leads to those inner questions and resentments which begin to foul up your relationship with God. After all, isn't it somewhat His fault that you are this way? He made you as you are. He could have and probably should have done it differently. But He didn't. So it probably means that though He cares for others and gives them a lot of things, He isn't really concerned about you. They're OK, but you're not.

However, once you become critical of the *design*, it isn't long until you feel resentful toward the *Designer*. This is how your concept of God becomes contaminated and your perception of how He feels about you gets all mixed up, finally ruining your relationship with Him.

Low self-esteem also spoils your relationships with other people. Satan uses your nagging sense of inferiority and inadequacy to isolate you. For the commonest way to cope with feelings of inferiority is to pull within yourself, to have as little contact with other people as you possibly can, and just occasionally to peek out as the rest of the world goes by.

Christ commanded us to love our neighbors as we love ourselves. This implies that it is basic to Christian ethics and to interpersonal relationships for a Christian to have a healthy self-image.

You are able to give to others only when you have a proper and healthy opinion of yourself. When you devalue yourself, you become overly absorbed *in* and *with* yourself, and you don't have anything left over to give to others.

Who are the hardest people to get along with? Those who don't like themselves. Because they don't like themselves, they don't like others, and they're hard to get along with. Low self-esteem wrecks interpersonal relationships more than anything else I know.

If you have low self-esteem, you ask another human being to do for you what no other person can do—to make you feel adequate and able—when you are already convinced that you are inadequate and unable. That puts too heavy a demand on husband or wife, on children, friends, neighbors, or church. You may become either suspicious and hostile, or cringing and clinging. God wants you to bloom with your own individual beauty, to do your part in making His garden colorful and beautiful.

PERSONAL REFLECTION

■ Take an honest inventory of your self-image. Would you describe your self-esteem as realistic and appropriate, or are you frequently self-critical and belittling? Describe ways in which inappropriate self-esteem is currently sabotaging your relationships.

_____

_____

_____

_____

■ In what ways have you been critical of your personal *design?* Have you ever complained to God about the way He made you? Look up Psalm 139 and read verses 1-18 and 23-24. David's song is a soothing reminder of the excellence of God's design in you. After reading this psalm, write a short response, expressing to God your feelings about yourself.

_____

_____

_____

_____

_____

_____

_____

4. Low self-esteem sabotages your Christian service. What's the greatest obstacle that prevents members of the body of Christ from functioning as parts of the body? What's the first thing people say when you ask them to do something in the body of Christ?

■ "Teach a Sunday School class? I can't stand up in front of people.

■ "Share at the women's meeting, or at the men's meeting? Oh, I couldn't do that.

■ "Go knocking on doors? That would scare me to death.

■ "Sing in the choir? Why don't you ask Mary? She has a much better voice."

We pastors are nearly drowned in the torrent of downgrading that pours over us in excuses for not doing God's work. I'm not talking about trying to put a square peg in a round hole. Not everybody can do everything. I know people in the church who say, "Pastor, I'm tongue-tied. Public speaking is not my gift, but I can do something else." Everybody can do something and function as a giver of his gift in the body of Christ.

Did you ever notice that God doesn't choose superstars to do His work? Check it out, all the way from Moses—who lost no time in telling God about his stuttering, to Mama's boy Mark—who ran out on Paul and Barnabas. Paul was right when he said that not many wise and noble and terrific are chosen. It seems that God takes people with shortcomings and infirmities, gives them work to do, and then supplies them with sufficient grace to do it. Not many wise, not many noble, not many supermen, not many wonderwomen are on this team (1 Cor. 1:26-31).

The trouble is that your low self-esteem robs God of marvelous opportunities to show off His power and ability through your weaknesses. Paul said, "Therefore, will I rather glory in my infirmities." Why? Because they gave God such a wonderful chance to show off His perfection (2 Cor. 12:9-10). Nothing sabotages Christian service more than thinking so little of yourself that you never really give God a chance.

PERSONAL REFLECTION

■ Have you ever been asked to do a work for God that you felt afraid to do? What was it? Did you do it? Explain why or why not.

_____

_____

_____

_____

_____

_____

■ In what ways has God shown off His power and ability through your weaknesses? Cite specific examples of how God has used your weaknesses to bring glory to Himself.

_____

_____

_____

_____

_____

_____

Do you remember the story about bazaar day in an Indian village? Everybody brought his wares to trade and sell. One farmer brought in a whole covey of quail. And he had tied a string around one foot of each bird. The other ends of all the strings were tied to a ring on a central stick. And the quail were dolefully walking in a circle, around and around, like mules at a sorghum mill. Nobody seemed interested in buying any quail, until along came a devout Brahman. He believed in the Hindu idea of respect for all life and his heart of compassion went out to these poor little creatures. The Brahman inquired the price of the quail and then said to the merchant, "I want to buy them all." The merchant was elated. After he received his money, he was surprised to hear the Brahman say, "Now I want you to set them all free."

"What's that, sir?"

"You heard me. Cut the strings off their feet and turn them loose. Set them all free."

"Well, all right, sir. If that will please you." With his knife the farmer cut the strings off the legs of the quail and set them free. What happened? The quail simply continued marching around and around in a circle. Finally, he had to shoo them off. Even when they landed some distance away, they resumed marching. Free, unbound, released, yet going around in circles as if still tied.

Are you in that picture? Freed, forgiven, a son, a daughter of God, a member of His family, but thinking of yourself as a worm or grasshopper? Low self-esteem is Satan's deadliest psychological weapon, and it can keep you marching around in vicious circles of fear and uselessness.

PRAYERFUL REFLECTION

■ Has Satan's deadliest psychological weapon, low self-esteem, got you going around in vicious circles of fear and uselessness? Then remember this: We are seen by God as being so precious that we are infinite in worth. How does that statement make you feel? Complete the following prayer, putting into words your feelings about God's unconditional acceptance of you.

Dear Lord Jesus,

Knowing You value me so much _____

_____

_____

_____

_____

_____

_____

_____

PERSONAL RENEWAL

■ The Psalmist David had a clear picture of how God saw him. Renew your thoughts and feelings this week by meditating on Psalm 139:1, 13-17.

Lord, You have examined me. You know all about me. . . .
You made my whole being. You formed me in my mother's
body. I praise You because You made me in an amazing and
wonderful way. What You have done is wonderful. I know
this very well. You saw my bones being formed as I took
shape in my mother's body. When I was put together
there, You saw my body as it was formed. All the days

for me were written in Your book before I was one day old. God, Your thoughts are precious to me. They are so many! (NCV)

Consider the incredible love that the Father has shown us in allowing us to be called "children of God"—and that is not just what we are called, but what we are. Our heredity on the Godward side is no mere figure of speech—which explains why the world will no more recognize us than it recognized Christ. Oh, dear children of mine (forgive the affection of an old man), have you realized it?

Here and now we are God's children. We don't know what we shall become in the future. We only know that, if reality were to break through, we should reflect His likeness, for we should see Him as He really is.

1 John 3:1-2, PH

Chapter 5
Healing Our Low
Self-Esteem—Part 1

Many years ago, a famous plastic surgeon, Dr. Maxwell Maltz, wrote a best-selling book, *New Faces—New Futures*. It was a collection of case histories of people for whom facial plastic surgery had opened the door to a new life. The author's theme was that amazing personality changes can take place when a person's face is changed.

However, as the years went by, Dr. Maltz began to learn something else, not from his successes but from his failures. He began to see patient after patient who, even after facial plastic surgery, did not change. People who were made not simply acceptable, but actually beautiful, kept on thinking and acting the part of the ugly duckling. They acquired new faces but went on wearing the same old personalities. Worse than that, when they looked in a mirror, they would angrily exclaim to the doctor, "I look the same as before. You didn't change a thing." This, in spite of the fact that their friends and their family members could hardly recognize them. Although before-and-after photographs were drastically different, Dr. Maltz's patients kept insisting, "My nose is the same," "My cheekbones are the same," "You didn't help at all."

In 1960 Dr. Maltz wrote his best-seller, *Psycho-Cybernetics* (Prentice-Hall). He was still trying to change people, not by correcting jutting jawbones, or smoothing out scars, but by helping them change the pictures they had of themselves.

Dr. Maltz says it is as if every personality has a face. This emotional face of personality seems to be the real key to change. If it remains scarred and distorted, ugly and inferior, then the person continues to act out a role, regardless of the change in his physical appearance. But if the face of his personality can be reconstructed, if the old emotional scars can be removed, the person can be changed.

All of us could confirm this by our experiences with people as well as our knowledge of ourselves. It is absolutely amazing the way self-image influences our actions and attitudes, and especially our relationships with other people.

Take Marie, for example. Marie's husband, Jim, thought his wife was beautiful. He told me so before they ever came to talk things over. When I saw her, I agreed with him. Jim liked to brag on her to others, and never tired of lovingly telling Marie that she was beautiful. He enjoyed buying her pretty clothes, little love gifts to make her look even more attractive. Now deep down, every wife wants this from her husband. But in Marie's case, her husband's admiration was causing problems, for Marie's picture of herself was diametrically opposite to what Jim saw.

"You're only saying that to flatter me," she'd say. "You don't really mean it."

Jim would feel hurt and frustrated. The more ways he tried to convince Marie that he really thought she was beautiful, the bigger the barrier became.

"I know what I look like," she said. "I can see myself in the mirror. You don't have to make up things like that. Why don't you love me for what I am?" And round and round it went.

Marie's self-concept kept her from thanking God for the gift of beauty. It prevented her from seeing reality. Worst of all, it hindered her from developing a beautiful love-gift relationship with her very devoted husband.

What is self-image or self-concept? Your self-image is based on a whole system of pictures and feelings you have put together about yourself. To express this combination of imagery and emotions, I often use the compound words *feeling-concepts* or *concept-feelings*. For self-concept includes both mental pictures and emotional feelings. You have a whole system of feeling-concepts and concept-feelings about yourself. This is at the very core of your personality. And nowhere is the biblical statement about the heart and mind more appropriate then here: "As he thinketh in his heart, so is he" (Prov. 23:7). The way you *look at* yourself and *feel about* yourself, way down deep in the heart of your personality—so you will be and so you will become. What you see and feel will determine your relationships both with people and with God.

PERSONAL REFLECTION

■ How do you see yourself? What feelings do you have about yourself? Use the picture space below to draw your answers to these two questions. Try drawing your pictures using the opposite hand with which you write.

PERSONAL
REFLECTION

■ At present, how is the way you *look at* and *feel about* yourself affecting your relationship with other people? Your relationship with God?

_____

_____

_____

_____

_____

Dr. Maurice Wagner, a professional Christian counselor, in his excellent book *The Sensation of Being Somebody* (Zondervan, pp.

32–37), explains the three essential components of a healthy self-image.

The first is *a sense of belongingness*, of being loved. This is simply the awareness of being wanted, accepted, cared for, enjoyed, and loved. I personally believe that this sense begins before birth. I've counseled people with such deep wounds that I am convinced their sense of rejection traces back to their parents' attitudes before birth. If a child is unwanted, rarely will he have a sense of belonging.

The second component is *a sense of worth and value*. This is the inner belief and feeling: "I count. I am of value. I have something to offer.

The third is *a sense of being competent*. It is the feeling-concept: "I can do this task; I can cope with that situation; I am able to meet life." Put them all together, Dr. Wagner says, and you have a triad of self-concept feelings: *belongingness*, *worthwhileness*, and *competence*.

TRIAD OF SELF-CONCEPT FEELINGS

PERSONAL
REFLECTION

■ Of the three components of a healthy self-image listed above, which one do you seem to wrestle with the most? Give an example of how your lack of a sense of *belongingness*, *worthwhileness*, or *competence* is impairing your life at present.

_____

_____

_____

_____

_____

_____

There are four sources of self-image, four factors which help a person construct self-image: *the outer world, the inner world, Satan with all the forces of evil,* and *God and His Word.* In this chapter we will look at the outer world since this is the primary source, the basic soil out of which our self-image grows.

Your outer world includes all the factors that have gone into your makeup—your inheritance and birth, your infancy, childhood, and teen years. Your outer world is your experience of life right up to the present time. Your experience with the outer world tells you how you were treated, how your were trained, and how you related to people in the early years of your life. It primarily reflects your parents and family members and the messages they sent to you about yourself through their facial expressions, tones, attitudes, words, and actions.

George Herbert Mead, a great social psychologist, uses an interesting phrase to describe a person's relationship to the outer world. He calls it the "looking-glass self." A baby has little concept of the self. But as he grows, he gradually comes to distinguish differences and to gain a pictue of himself. Where does he get it? From the reflection of the reactions of the important other people in his life.

PERSONAL REFLECTION

■ List the names of the significant others who were part of your life between the ages of 0 and 12. Between the ages of 13 and 19. From age 20 to present.

_____

_____

_____

_____

■ What messages do you remember these important people sending to you about yourself through their facial expressions, tones, attitudes, words, and actions when you were a child? A teenager? An adult? List as many things as you can recall.

_____

_____

_____

_____

_____

_____

_____

Saint Paul was centuries ahead of Dr. Mead. At the heart of the Love Chapter, 1 Corinthians 13 (vv. 9-12), Paul used the same idea when he spoke of growing up:

My knowledge is imperfect, including my knowledge about myself. When I was a child, I spoke and thought and reasoned like a child. When I grew up I put away my childish ways, and yet even so I still see as in a mirror that offers me only reflections. But one day I'll have perfect knowledge. Then I'll see God and reality face-to-face. Now I know in part, but I will then understand myself fully, even as I have been fully understood. My present partial understanding comes because I see myself in a mirror darkly and dimly. (Author's paraphrase)

One of the characteristics of the child is that he knows and understands things partially. Part of growing up into mature love is to reach a fuller, face-to-face understanding. Our pictures and our feelings about ourselves come largely from the pictures and the feelings we see reflected in our family members—what we watch in their expressions, hear from the tone in their voices, and see from their actions. These reflections tell us not only who we are, but also what we are going to become. As the reflections gradually become part of us, we take on the shape of the person we see in the family looking glass.

Do you remember the last time you went into the house of mirrors in an amusement park? You looked in one mirror and saw yourself as tall and skeletal, with foot-long hands. In the next one, you were round like a big balloon. Another mirror combined both, so that from the waist up you looked like a giraffe, while from the waist down you looked like a hippopotamus.

Looking into the mirrors was a hilarious experience, especially for the person standing next to you. He was just knocked out at how funny you looked. What was happening? The mirrors were so constructed that you saw yourself according to the curvature of the glass.

Now, move those mirrors over into the family. What if somehow your mother, your dad, your brother, your sister, your grandparents, the important others in your life—what if they had taken every mirror in the house and curved them a certain way, so that in every mirror you saw a distorted reflection of yourself? What would have happened? It wouldn't have taken you long to develop an image of yourself just like the one you were seeing in the family mirrors. After a while you would have begun talking and acting and relating to people in a way that would have fit the picture you kept seeing in those mirrors.

At our Ashram retreats we have a session called "The Hour of the Open Heart," when people openly share their deepest needs. The question of the hour is, "What is it in your life that keeps you from being your best for Jesus Christ?" One evening a minister got up to share. He was in his early forties, handsome, successful, in the prime of life. He was pastor of a large and growing church. But he confessed with deep emotion his nagging fears of inadequacy, his constant battle with inferiority. He was too sensitive to what people said about him and found himself freezing up at the slightest criticism. His fear kept him from launching out in creative ministries to which he felt God was leading him.

After that open-heart session, a church leader said to me, "You know, that minister is the last person in the world I ever expected to hear say that. Why, he is so handsome and so successful. He's got a great family and a marvelous church. I would never have guessed that such torment would go on in that man's heart."

I happened to know the minister's family. I knew the way he had been neglected by his father—and that "mirror" tells a kid a lot. If a dad doesn't have time for his child, he reflects an important message: "You're not worth my time; I've got more important things to do." I knew of the constant put-downs from his father, and the honeyed, syrupy, spiritual way his mother was always trying to help him. Her way of helping was to remind him of what was expected of him, or to compare him with a very bright, and attractive older sister. I knew the destructively curved mirrors of neglect and lack of affection, and the criticism and comparison in which his self-esteem had been badly distorted. Those hurts and those wounds were infecting his personality thirty years later, paralyzing his potential, and sabotaging his service for God.

In case this sounds as if I am looking for someone on whom to place the blame, let me say that indeed I am not. In this fallen and imperfect world, all parents are imperfect in parenting. Most parents I know do the very best they can. Unfortunately, the role models they had weren't so hot either, all the way back to Adam and Eve. Cain and Abel must have seen a lot of conflict and tension: theirs must have been an unhappy home, for one brother to end up killing the other.

Though all of us are guilty, I am not trying to assess blame. Rather, I am trying to help us gain insight and understanding so we can find where we need healing, where we need to reconstruct a proper self-esteem.

PERSONAL
REFLECTION

■ The first step toward healing damaged emotions is *to acknowledge* past wrongs that were done to you. (This does not mean that you look for someone to blame.) The truth is—those who do not remember the past are doomed to repeat it. In what ways have you resisted acknowledging wrongs from the past? Write a few sentences of "self-talk" which reveal how you feel about acknowledging painful past experiences.

_____

_____

_____

_____

_____

_____

Do you need a new set or mirrors for yourself? So many teenagers do, and so do young couples as they bring up their children. Someone has said, "Your childhood is the time of life when God desires to build the rooms of the temple in which He wants to live when you are an adult." What a beautiful thought! Parents have the great privilege, *and* heavy responsibility, of giving the basic design to the temple—the child's self-image.

If he is convinced he is of low worth, a child will place little value on what he says or does. If he is programmed for incompetence, he will be incompetent. One man told me that the thing he remembers more than anything else is the way his father always said to him, "I tell you, if there's a wrong way to do it, you'll find it."

If this kind of low-self-esteem has been programmed into a person, it is difficult, and in some cases almost impossible, for that person to feel beloved of God, accepted by Him, and of worth to Him in His kingdom and service. A great many seemingly spiritual struggles are not spiritual at all in their origin. Although they sound and act and feel like God's judgment on a guilty conscience, they actually come from damning and damaging feeling-concepts that cause low self-esteem.

That was the case with Shirley, the wife of a seminarian. She was about twenty-five when she came for help. When Shirley began to pour out her pain, it came in a torrent. She had marriage problems by the bucketful and tensions in her work. She'd already changed jobs several times because of difficulties in getting along with people. In spite of the sincerest attempts at devotions, witnessing, Christian work, and prayer, she was not at all happy with her relationship with God and was sure God was not at all happy with her.

She had been given many good things by her parents in their rural home—security, hard work, discipline, strong Christian commitment, and high standards of morality. Shirley's parents were salt-of-the-earth folks, and from them she had gained a sincere though dutiful love for God and His Word and the church.

But gradually Shirley and I began to see that though her parents had done their best, they'd gone at it the wrong way, by giving compliments that made comparisons or set conditions.

- "Shirley, you're so nice when . . ."
- "Shirley, I hope you'll never be like Sally down the road."
- "That's fine, Shirley, but . . ."
- "We love you when . . . if . . . but . . ."

So many conditions! And Shirley grew up outdoing herself, performing, working, striving, and achieving. And she did remarkably well, except in one area. You know how some girls during adolescence go through an "ugly duckling" stage. Shirley was one of these, and her dad tried to help her accept herself. He really did love her, but again and again he said to her, "You know, you just can't make a peach out of a potato." While he thought he was helping her, he was really scarring and cutting at the very heart of her self-esteem. She grew up with a potato self, thinking of herself as misshapen, ugly, as something that grew under the ground.

PERSONAL REFLECTION

- In what ways do you relate to Shirley's story? Write a little bit about your own story below if it at all resembles Shirley's.

_____

_____

_____

_____

_____

_____

_____

Shirley and I began to see that the potato image had affected everything in her life, had made her as sensitive as an open wound.

She took everything wrong that was said to her by her friends, her boss, her fellow workers, her neighbors, and her loving husband. And, of course, her God. How could she believe God loved her if He had made her a potato? It wasn't very nice of Him to do that, was it? Neither could she accept her husband's love. We like potatoes to eat, but their appearance leaves something to be desired.

The hurts Shirley suffered were deep. We had to walk through those painful memories with our Lord, turning them over to Him for healing. All during the long time we counseled together, I rarely used Shirley's name. I often called her "God's Peach" or "My Peach."

I went out of my way to reprogram her self-image. And she responded to the grace of God in such a marvelous way. When she discovered she was a daughter of God, she let love and grace pour in and wash away all those potato feelings and potato images. It was one of the most remarkable changes I have ever seen. Her very appearance changed. As Shirley began caring for herself, she started to look more attractive. Better still, she became an attractive person and began to relate better to people. She became a human being with proper Christian self-worth.

Some years later when I was a guest speaker in another state, Shirley came up to me after the service, holding the most precious baby—a real beauty. I looked at that little girl and said, "Shirley, no potato ever produced that." She looked at me with a mischievous smile and laughingly said, "Pretty peachy, huh?"

PRAYERFUL
REFLECTION

■ John in his first letter to the church reminds the saints that they are called "children of God"—not just so, but that they indeed ARE CHILDREN OF GOD. Think for a moment about what it means to be a child of God. How does that make you feel about yourself? Write a short letter-prayer to God telling Him how you feel about Him being your Father and your being His daughter/son.

_____

_____

_____

_____

_____

_____

PERSONAL RENEWAL

■ Renew your thoughts and feelings this week by meditating on J. B. Phillips' paraphrase of 1 John 3:1-2.

> *Consider the incredible love that the Father has shown us in allowing us to be called "children of God"—and that is not just what we are called, but what we are. Our heredity on the Godward side is no mere figure of speech— which explains why the world will no more recognize us than it recognized Christ. Oh, dear children of mine (forgive the affection of an old man), have you realized it? Here and now we are God's children. We don't know what we shall become in the future. We only know that, if reality were to break through, we should reflect His likeness, for we should see Him as He really is.*

In human experience it is a rare thing for one man to give his life for another, even if the latter be a good man, though there have been a few who have had the courage to do it. Yet the proof of God's amazing love is this: that it was while we were sinners that Christ died for us. Moreover, if He did that for us while we were sinners, now that we are men justified by the shedding of His blood, what reason have we to fear the wrath of God?

If while we were His enemies, Christ reconciled us to God by dying for us, surely now that we are reconciled we may be perfectly certain of our salvation through His living in us. "Nor, I am sure, is this a matter of bare salvation—we may hold our heads high in the light of God's love because of the reconciliation which Christ has made.

Romans 5:7-11, PH

Thou shalt love the Lord thy God with all thy heart, and with all thy soul, and with all thy mind. This is the first and great commandment. And the second is like unto it, "Thou shalt love thy neighbor as thyself." On these two comandments hang all the Law and Prophets.

Matthew 22:37-40

Chapter 6
Healing Our Low Self-Esteem—Part 2

A person's self-concept is a system of feelings and concepts he has constructed about himself. There are four sources from which we get our self-concepts.

FOUR SOURCES OF SELF-CONCEPT

The first is the outer world, that we looked at in chapter 5. From this outer world we see pictures and feelings about ourselves reflected in the mirrors of family members. We decide who we are from our earliest system of relationships—by how we are treated and loved and cared for, and the language of relationships that we learn as we are growing up.

The second source is the world within us, the physical, emotional, and spiritual equipment that we bring into the world. This includes our senses, our nerves, our capacity to learn, to register, to respond. For some of us, the world within includes handicaps, deformities, and defects.

No two children are alike. They are as marvelously different as snowflakes. And what a mistake parents make in going by any book to raise their children as if they were all alike. You parents know what I'm talking about. You've got one child who's so much like the proverbial mule that you may have to use a two-by-four just to get his attention, let alone discipline him. And then you have another child who is as sensitive as a touch-me-not plant—you don't have to raise a hand or a voice to get response. How ridiculous to think that one set of child-rearing principles is enough. These differences exist because of who we are and because of our psychophysical equipment.

However, there is also a spiritual factor. And it is at this point that we differ with all secular, humanistic, and pagan psychology, which looks at human nature as essentially good or morally neutral. We Christians do not do that. God has revealed to us in His Word that we do not enter this life morally neutral. Rather, we are victims of a basic tendency toward evil, a proclivity toward the wrong. We call it original sin.

The truth is that sin is the one thing about all of us that is not very original. The laws and the principles which govern all personal relationships and human development guaranteed sin's transmission, when our first set of parents got out of sorts with God and began living in self-centeredness and pride. Beginning with the first sin of Adam and Eve, there was set in motion a chain reaction of imperfect parenting, through failures and ignorance and misguided actions and, worst of all, through conditional love.

This parental inheritance makes every human being a victim of corporate sinfulness. We do not come into this world perfectly neutral, but imperfectly weighted in the direction of the wrong. We are out of balance in our motives, desires, and drives. We are out of proportion, with a bent toward the wrong. And because of this defect in our natures, our responses are off-center.

PERSONAL REFLECTION

■ In Romans 7:14, the Apostle Paul lays out the sin-nature dilemma we all struggle with when he says, "I do not understand the things I do. I do not do the good things I want to do. And I do the bad things I hate to do" (NCV). In what areas of your life do you most often find yourself being "bent toward the wrong"? Describe a time recently when you found yourself in just the predicament Paul talks about in Romans 7:14.

Years ago I found a saying that is extremely helpful in counseling people: "Children are the world's greatest recorders, but they are the world's worst interpreters." Kids pick up many of the imperfections around them and, because of the self-centeredness which is in all of us, they misinterpret much of what they take in, and this greatly affects their self-image. Regardless of how well parents do by their children, it seems that most people reach young adulthood feeling, "You're OK but I'm not OK." It is almost a part of our human equipment.

The Bible makes it clear that we are not merely victims. We all are sinners and share in the responsibility of who we are and what we are becoming. I have never seen anyone truly healed until along with forgiving all those who hurt and wronged him, he also received God's forgiveness for his own wrong responses.

Satan is a third source, and we have already considered him as a source of our low self-esteem. Satan uses our feelings of self-despising as a terrible weapon in three roles that he plays. Satan is a liar (John 8:44), the accuser (Rev. 12:10), and the one who blinds our minds (2 Cor. 4:4). In all three roles he uses inferiority, inadequacy, and self-belittling to defeat Christians and prevent them from realizing their full potential as God's own children.

PERSONAL REFLECTION

■ Think of a time recently when Satan, the accuser, played on your low self-esteem and you felt shamed and belittled for something you had done. Write a little bit about that experience in the space provided below. *EXAMPLE: I told our youth pastor, Bill, that he could use our home to host a parents' meeting. But I forgot to check with my wife until it was too late. When Bill approached me to confirm his meeting plans, I told him my wife had already made other plans for that evening and that our home would not be available. I was surprised at how quickly I excused myself with a lie because I was afraid to admit that I had failed to do what I said I would. I certainly don't feel like much of a Christian!*

_____

_____

_____

_____

_____

The fourth source for our self-concept is God. We now move from the problem of low self-image to the power for a new Christian self-image. We now turn away from the disease to its cure, for there are practical steps you can take toward the healing of your low self-esteem.

Let God and His Word straighten out your false beliefs. Many Christians have adopted an idea which is really a sin in God's sight, and have wrapped it in pious theological garb. You too may have made a virtue out of a vice. Now you cannot at the same time think wrongly and live rightly. You cannot believe error and practice truth.

The truth is that self-belittling is not true Christian humility and runs counter to some very basic teachings of the Christian faith. The great commandment is that you love God with all your being. The second commandment is an extension of the first—that you love your neighbor as you love yourself. We do not have two commandments here, but three: to love God, to love yourself, and to love others. I put *self* second, because Jesus plainly made a proper self-love the basis of a proper love for neighbor. The term *self-love* has a wrong connotation for some people. Whether you call it self-esteem or self-worth, it is plainly the foundation of Christian love for others. And this is the opposite of what many Christians believe.

PERSONAL REFLECTION

■ What connotation does the term *self-love* hold for you? Describe what self-love looks like to you.

_____

_____

_____

_____

Years ago, after I preached a sermon about these two great commandments of Jesus, a man came up to me. He said, "As old as I am, I have never before actually heard Jesus' Word correctly."

I said, "What do you mean?"

"Well," he said, "while you were preaching, I suddenly realized that with my lips I have said, 'Love thy neighbor as thyself,' but deep down in my inner self I have really been hearing, 'Love thy neighbor but hate thyself.' I'm afraid I have been scrupulously living up to the commandment as I translated it."

After a revival meeting when I preached about proper self-love, a woman came to me and said that she had been in the church all her life, but that I was the first evangelist she had ever heard say that she was supposed to love herself. "All this time I thought that God wanted me to dislike myself in order to stay humble."

PERSONAL REFLECTION

■ In Philippians 2:3, the Apostle Paul writes, "Do nothing out of selfish ambition or vain conceit, but in humility consider others better than yourselves." What is your understanding of this verse? Have you been taught that to stay humble you have to dislike yourself? How has this kind of thinking impacted your ability to love yourself? Your ability to love God?

_____

_____

_____

_____

_____

_____

Do you need to get your theology straightened out? When you love God and yourself and others, you are fulfilling the whole law of God (Matt. 5:43-48). As Jesus proclaimed the law, He was not endorsing or glorifying it, as some rabbis of His day used to do. Rather He was authoritatively restating the principle of the eternal triangle—proper love for God, for ourselves, and for other people. This basic law of God is written into the nature of the entire universe. It operates in every cell of your body. The person who has proper self-esteem is healthier in every way than the person with low self-esteem. This is the way God has made you, and if you go against this, you are not only following wrong theology, but bargaining with your own destruction.

Although many Scriptures suggest the importance of high self-esteem, the Apostle Paul directly declared it to be the basis of one of the most intimate and important relationships of life—that of husband and wife in marriage: "Husbands ought also to love their wives as their own bodies. He who loves his own wife loves himself; for no one ever hated his own flesh, but nourishes and cherishes it" (Eph. 5:28-29, NASB).

Phillips paraphrased it by saying, "The love a man gives his wife is the extending of his love for himself to enfold her." The divine example is given in the next verse. "And that is what Christ does for His body, the church." And then Paul stated it again: "Let every one of you who is a husband love his wife as he loves himself, and let the wife reverence her husband."

Experience confirms Paul's psychological accuracy. Because some people love their partners the way they love themselves their marriages are in trouble. For self-belittling works its way out through marriage. A proper self-nourishing and a realization of your own worth are essential if you are to be a good wife or husband.

Such self-esteem is essential to being a good neighbor. Paul's caution is appropriate, that each believer would not think of himself more highly than he ought to, but would think with sober judgment (Rom. 12:3). Sober judgment neither overestimates nor underestimates. It is Satan who confuses and blinds us at this point, as he accuses, "Look out, now; you're feeling proud."

But really the opposite is true. For the person with low self-esteem is always trying to prove himself. He has a need to be right in every situation, to verify himself. He gets all wrapped up in constantly looking at himself.

A person with low self-esteem becomes extremely self-centered. This doesn't necessarily mean he is selfish. He may be a doormat, and this is part of his problem. But he is self-centered in that he is always looking at himself and wondering about himself. He may even become a praise-aholic, constantly maneuvering others into reassuring him.

You cannot really unconditionally love others when you need to prove your own self-worth. It nay look as if you are loving them, when actually you are just using them to reassure yourself that you're OK.

Self-negation is not a part of humility or holiness or sanctification. Self-crucifixion and self-surrender do not mean the downgrading of self.

PERSONAL REFLECTION

■ Do you have a tendency to either overestimate or underestimate your own value and abilities as a person? Make a list of any "non-sober" thoughts you've had about yourself in the past couple of weeks. Is it difficult for you to stay honest with yourself about yourself? Why?

_____

_____

_____

_____

_____

_____

■ What are some things you do to nourish or love yourself? How has proper self-nourishing made a difference in your ability to "love your neighbor (your spouse, children, friend, employer) as yourself"? What happens when you don't properly nourish yourself?

_____

_____

_____

_____

Develop the picture of your worth and value from God, not from the false reflections that come out of your past. The healing of low self-esteem really hinges on a choice you must make: Will you listen to Satan as he employs all the lies, the distortions, the put-downs, and the hurts of your past to keep you bound by unhealthy, unchristian feelings and concepts about yourself? Or will you receive your self-esteem from God and His Word?

Here are some very important questions to ask yourself.

What right have you to belittle or despise someone whom God loves so deeply? Don't say, "Well, I know God loves me, but I just can't stand myself." That's a travesty of faith, an insult to God and His love. It is the expression of a subtly hidden resentment against your Creator. When you despise His creation, you are really saying that you don't like the design or care much for the Designer. You are calling unclean what God calls clean. You are failing to realize how much God loves you and how much you mean to Him.

What right have you to belittle or despise someone whom God has honored so highly? "Consider the incredible love that the Father has shown us in allowing us to be called 'children of God'" (1 John 3:1, PH). And that's not just what we're called. It's what we are. "Oh, dear children of mine . . . have you realized it? Here and now we are God's children" (v. 2, PH).

Do you think that when you consider God's son or daughter worthless or inferior, He is pleased by your so-called humility?

What right have you to belittle or despise someone who God values so highly? How much does God value you? "In human experience it is a rare thing for one man to give his life for another, even if the latter be a good man. . . . Yet the proof of God's amazing love is this: that it was while we were sinners that Christ died for us. . . . We may hold our heads high in the light of God's love" (Rom. 5:7-8, 11, PH). God has declared your value. You are someone who God values so highly as to give the life of His own dear Son to redeem you.

What right have you to belittle or despise someone whom God has provided for so fully? "How much more shall your Father which is in heaven give good things?" (Matt. 7:11) "God shall supply all your need" (Phil. 4:19). This doesn't sound as if He wants you to be self-loathing or to feel inadequate.

What right have you to belittle or despise someone whom God has planned for so carefully? "Praise be to God . . . for giving us through Christ every spiritual benefit. . . . Consider what He has done—before the foundation of the world He chose us to become in Christ, His holy and blameless children, living within His constant care. He planned, in His purposeful love, that we should be adopted as His own children" (Eph. 1:3-5, PH).

What right have you to belittle or despise someone in whom God delights? The Apostle Paul said that we are "accepted in the beloved" (Eph. 1:6). Do you remember the Father's words at the baptism of Jesus? "This is My beloved Son in whom I am well pleased" (Matt. 3:17). Paul gives us a daring thought: we are "in Christ." He used this phrase some ninety times. You are in Christ, therefore you are in the Beloved. God looks at you in Christ and says to you, "You are My beloved son, you are My beloved daughter, in whom I am well pleased."

From where will you get your idea of yourself? From distortions of your childhood? From past hurts and false ideas that have been programmed into you? Or will you say, "No, I will not listen to those lies from the past any longer. I will not listen to Satan, the liar, the confuser, the blinder, who twists and distorts. I am going to listen to God's opinion of me, and let Him reprogram me until His loving estimate of me becomes a part of my life, right down to my innermost feelings."

You must become a partner with God in this reprogramming and renewal process. Such work is a continuous process, not a sudden crisis. I don't know of any single Christian experience that will change your self-image overnight. You are to be "transformed by the renewing of your mind" (Rom. 12:2). The verbs in this verse represent continuous action, and the word *mind* describes the way you think, the way you look at life as a daily process.

PERSONAL REFLECTION

■ Are you ready to give up your old, destructive ways of seeing yourself and become a partner with God in reprogramming and renewing the way you think? If so, then try this **Daily Affirmations** exercise. Read the list of affirmation statements below every morning when you awaken and again at night before you go to sleep. They will remind you of the wonderful ways in which God sees YOU.

Daily Affirmations

■ Lord Jesus, I know You **love** me. Thank You for making me in an amazing and wonderful way. What You have created is precious.

■ Thank You, Father, for calling me Your child. Knowing this gives me a sense of being **honored**.

■ God, You declared Your **value** of me when You gave the life of Your Son, Jesus, to redeem me. Thank You for valuing me so highly.

■ Jesus, You have promised to supply all my needs according to Your riches. Today I choose to trust You with every need that I have. Thank You for **providing** for me so fully.

■ Lord, even before the foundation of the world You chose to adopt me as Your own child. Thank You for having **planned** for me so carefully.

■ God, thank You for looking at me in Christ and declaring me accepted and beloved. It is awesome to think that You are **delighted** in me.

How can you cooperate with the Holy Spirit to accomplish the process of renewal in your life?

Ask God to check you every time you belittle yourself. When you start doing this, you're in for a surprise. For you may find that your whole lifestyle is a direct or indirect put-down of yourself. Here are a few hints. What do you do when someone compliments you? Can you say "Thank you"? "I'm glad you liked that"? "I appreciate that"? Or do you go into a long song and dance of cutting yourself down? If you have been belittling yourself, it'll tear you up for a while to stop, because you'll want to go through the whole routine. Don't do it.

I think the spiritualizing is the worst; it must be nauseating to God. Someone says, "I heard you sing today and I enjoyed your song." Then do you become very spiritual and say, "Well, it really wasn't me; it was the Lord"? Sure, it was the Lord; you are dependent on Him. But you don't need to say that every time.

Let God love you, and let Him teach you how to love yourself and how to love others. You want love. You want God to affirm and accept you, and that's what He does. But because of wretched programming from the other sources, it is difficult to accept love. In fact, it is so hard that you may think it is more comfortable to go on just the way you are.

I challenge you to enter the healing process, so that you can lift your head high as a son or a daughter of God Himself.

PERSONAL REFLECTION

■ Throughout the week, make a list of times when you belittle yourself. Make a note below each time it happens.

_____

_____

_____

_____

■ Let God love you this week through other people. Use the space below to record any instances when God uses other people in your life to show you how much He loves, affirms, and accepts you.

_____

_____

_____

_____

PRAYERFUL REFLECTION

■ Healing your low self-esteem is not something that will happen overnight. This process of change takes place over a long period of time in cooperation with the Holy Spirit. Are you ready to enter the healing process? Complete the prayer of commitment below if you are ready to begin.

Holy Spirit,

Thank You for Your presence in my life. Help me not to listen to the lies from the past any longer, nor to listen to Satan, the liar, the confuser, the blinder, who twists and distorts the truth. Rather, I choose to listen to Your opinion of me and ask that You reprogram me until Your loving estimate of me becomes a part of my life, right down to my innermost feelings. I . . .

_____

_____

_____

PERSONAL RENEWAL

■ Begin to renew your self-esteem this week by meditating on Romans 12:1-2 (NIV). Keep in mind that the verbs in this verse represent continuous action—it is ongoing—and that the word *mind* describes the way you think, the way you look at life as a daily process.

> *Therefore, I urge you, brothers, in view of God's mercy, to offer your bodies as living sacrifices, holy and pleasing to God—this is your spiritual act of worship. Do not conform any longer to the pattern of this world, but be transformed by the renewing of your mind. Then you will be able to test and approve what God's will is—His good, pleasing, and perfect will.*

Come unto Me, all ye that labor and are heavy laden, and I will give you rest. Take My yoke upon you, and learn of Me; for I am meek and lowly in heart; and ye shall find rest unto your souls. For My yoke is easy, and My burden is light.

Matthew 11:28-30

There remaineth therefore a rest to the people of God. For he that is entered into his rest, he also hath ceased from his own works, as God did from His. Let us labor therefore to enter into that rest.

Hebrews 4:9-11

Chapter 7
Symptoms of Perfectionism

There are many different kinds of depression, and they vary greatly in degree. I am going to focus on a kind of depression caused by damaged emotions, and specifically by a spiritual distortion known as *perfectionism*.

Now the moment I mention that word, some red flags of defense go up. Isn't it a fact that we believe in Christian perfection? Indeed, we do. But there is a great difference between true Christian perfection and perfectionism. While on the surface they may look alike, there is a great gulf fixed between the two.

Perfectionism is a counterfeit for Christian perfection, holiness, sanctification, or the Spirit-filled life. Instead of making us holy persons and integrated personalities—that is, whole persons in Christ—perfectionism leaves us spiritual Pharisees and emotional neurotics.

PERSONAL REFLECTION

■ Go back and reread the first three paragraphs. Do the ideas expressed in those paragraphs make sense to you? Briefly explain why in the space below.

_____

_____

_____

_____

You think I'm exaggerating the picture? That this is some newfangled discovery by psychologists or the pastor? I want to assure you that throughout the centuries, sensitive pastors observed these kinds of suffering Christians, and were deeply concerned, long before the word *psychology* was ever in popular use. Although they didn't know what to do about it, they recognized the problem.

John Fletcher, a contemporary of John Wesley, described certain of his parishioners: Some bind heavy burdens on themselves of their own making and when they cannot bear them, they are tormented in their consciences with imaginary guilt. Others go distracted through groundless fears of having committed the unpardonable sin. In a word, do we not see hundreds who, when they have reason to think well of their state, instead think there is no hope for them whatever?

The itinerant pastor, John Wesley, recorded it this way:

"Sometimes this excellent quality, tenderness of conscience, is carried to an extreme. We find some who fear where no fear is, who are continually condemning themselves without cause, imagining something to be sinful where Scripture nowhere condemns it, supposing other things to be their duty where Scripture nowhere enjoins it. This is properly termed a scrupulous conscience, and is a sore evil. It is highly expedient to yield to it as little as possible, rather it is a matter of prayer that you may be delivered from this sore evil and may recover a sound mind" (Arthur C. Zepp, *Conscience Alone Not a Safe Guide,* Chicago: The Christian Witness Company, 1913, p. 103).

One ancient minister actually wrote a book about perfectionism, called *The Spiritual Treatment of Sufferers from Nerves and Scruples.* An amazingly accurate title!

Perfectionism is the most disturbing emotional problem among evangelical Christians. It walks into my office more often than any other single Christian hangup.

What is perfectionism? Since it is a lot easier to describe than to define, I want you to see some of its symptoms.

1. Tyranny of the oughts. Its chief characteristic is a constant overall feeling of never doing well enough or being good enough. This feeling permeates all of life, but especially affects our spiritual lives. Psychologist Karen Horney's classic phrase describes it perfectly, "The tyranny of the *oughts.*" Here are its typical statements:

- "I ought to do better,"
- "I ought to have done better,"
- "I ought to be able to do better."

All the way from preparing a meal to praying or witnessing—"I didn't do it quite well enough."

SYMPTOMS OF PERFECTIONISM

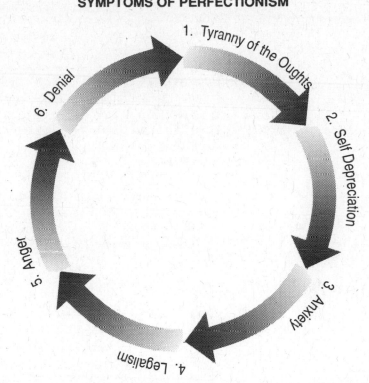

The three favorite phrases of the perfectionist are: "could have," "should have," "would have." If you are living in this emotional state, the official state song is "If Only." Always standing on tiptoe, always reaching, stretching, trying but never quite making it.

PERSONAL REFLECTION

■ Are you plagued by the "tyranny of the oughts"? Monitor your perfectionistic thinking this week by recording any instances when you catch yourself using the phrases, "could have," "should have," "would have," or "if only."

_____

_____

_____

_____

2. Self-depreciation. The connection between perfectionism and low self-esteem is obvious. If you are never quite good enough, you feel a continuous sense of self-depreciation. If you are never quite satisfied with yourself and your achievements, then the next step is quite natural: God is never really pleased with you either. He's always saying, "Come on now, you can do better than that!" And if you are a perfectionist and never pleased with yourself anyway, you reply, "Of course."

Try as you will, you always remain in second, not first place. And since you and God always demand first place, that's not quite good enough. So, back to the spiritual salt mines you go, with increased efforts to please yourself and an increasingly demanding God who is never quite satisfied. But you always fall short, you are inadequate, you never arrive but you must never stop trying.

PERSONAL REFLECTION

■ What behaviors in your life might indicate that you are holding on to a subtle belief that God is a "relentless taskmaster" and no matter how much you do or how well you do it, it will never quite be enough to keep Him happy?

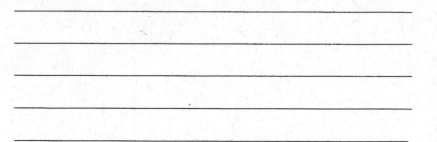

_____

_____

_____

_____

_____

3. Anxiety. The oughts and self-depreciation produce an oversensitive conscience under a giant umbrella of guilt, anxiety, and condemnation. Like a great cloud, the umbrella hangs over your head. Once in a while it lifts and the sun shines through, particularly during revivals, deeper life conferences, and retreats, when you go forward for prayer or "make a deeper surrender."

Unfortunately, the sunshine lasts about as long as it did the last time you made the same trip, went through the same process, and claimed the same blessing. Soon you fall off spiritual cloud nine with a sickening thud. Those same dreaded feelings settle in again. The general sense of divine disapproval, and comprehensive condemnation return, nagging and knocking at the back door of your soul.

PERSONAL REFLECTION

■ Do you recall ever attending a retreat or revival meeting where you experienced a "spiritual high" and "recommitted" your life to the Lord, only to find yourself shortly thereafter struggling with the same old feelings of divine disapproval and condemnation? Describe the "before" and "after" of that experience using as many

SYMPTOMS OF PERFECTIONISM / 109

feeling words as come to mind.

_____

_____

_____

_____

_____

4. Legalism. The oversensitive conscience and comprehensive guilt of the perfectionist are usually accompanied by a great scrupulosity and legalism which rigidly overemphasize externals, do's and don'ts, rules and regulations. Let's see why this almost inevitably follows the first three symptoms.

The perfectionist with his fragile conscience, his low self-esteem, and his almost built-in sense of automatic guilt is very sensitive to what other people think about him. Since he cannot accept himself, and is quite unsure of God's approval, he desperately needs the approval of other people. Thus he is easy prey to the opinions and evaluations of other Christians. Every sermon gets to him. He introspects: *Ah-h, maybe that's what's wrong with me. Maybe if I give this up . . . add that to my life . . . Maybe if I stop doing this or start doing that, I will experience peace, joy, and power. Maybe then God will accept me, and I will please Him.*

All the while, the do's and don'ts are piling up; they keep adding up because more and more people have to be pleased. The halo has to be adjusted for this person and readjusted for that one. So the perfectionist keeps fitting it this way and that way and, before he realizes what is happening, the halo has turned into what Paul called "the yoke of bondage" (Gal. 5:1). The yoke was a very familiar farm implement in those days, put upon an animal to pull the plow or to join two oxen together. But the word was used in another way, and this is the meaning Paul had in mind. In the Old Testament the yoke was a symbol of the despotic authority laid upon the necks of a conquered people as a symbol of their enslavement. It was something humiliating and destructive.

PERSONAL REFLECTION

■ In their book, *The Subtle Power of Spiritual Abuse*, authors David Johnson and Jeff VanVonderen make the point that "Churches are meant to be safe places where spiritual leaders help and equip the members for the work of service. There are some churches, however, where leaders use their spiritual authority to control and dominate others, attempting to meet their own needs for importance, power, intimacy, or spiritual gratification. Through the subtle use of the right "spiritual" words, church members are manipulated or shamed into certain behaviors or performance that ensnares in legalism, guilt, and begrudging service. This is *spiritual abuse*, and the results can be shattering. Deeply ingrained spiritual codes of written and unwritten rules control and condemn, wounding believers' spirits and keeping them from the grace and joy of God's kingdom. Believers find themselves enslaved to a system, a leader, a standard of performance that saps true spiritual life" (*The Subtle Power of Spiritual Abuse*, Bethany House, 1991). What kind of spiritual system (church and/or family) did you grow up in? Describe it. Did it overemphasize externals—the do's and don'ts, rules and regulations of the faith?

_____

_____

_____

_____

- In what ways is the spiritual system you are part of today similar to the one you grew up in? In what ways is it different?

_____

_____

_____

_____

- Dr. Seamands alludes to the Old Testament's understanding of a yoke. A yoke represented *enslavement, humiliation,* and *destruction* for those who came under it. What kind of spiritual "yokes" have you been carrying throughout your life? Name some of them.

_____

_____

_____

_____

_____

_____

The Good News is that the way to God is not the path of perfect performance. No matter how much you try, you can never *win* God's favor. Why? Because His favor, His being pleased with you, is a love-gift of His grace through Jesus Christ.

After a while, grace seemed *too good* to be true to the Galatians, and they began to listen to other voices in the marketplace; "another gospel" as Paul termed it (Gal. 1:6). Maybe they listened to *the Jerusalem legalists*, who said you had to keep all the law, including the ceremonial law. Maybe they listened to *the Colossian ascetics* who majored in giving up things in order to please God. They also majored in observing special days, new moons, and Sabbaths. They insisted on "self-abasement," and deliberate low self-esteem (Col. 2:18, NASB). How accurate!

And so, the Jerusalem legalists and the Colossians ascetics produced *the Galatian diluter, the Galatian reversionists.* They reverted to a diluted mixture of faith and works, law and grace. And the result was the same then as it is today when we mix law and grace. Immature and sensitive believers can become neurotic perfectionists who are guilt-ridden, tight-haloed, unhappy, and uncomfortable. They are rigid in their outlook, frigid in their lovelessness, conforming to the approval and disapproval of others. Yet, in a strange paradox, they critically judge, blame, and bind those same others.

5. Anger. But the worst is yet to come. For you see, something terrible is beginning to happen to the perfectionist. He may not realize it but deep in his heart a kind of anger is developing. A resentment against the oughts, against the Christian faith, against other Christians, against himself, but saddest of all, against God.

Oh, not that it's really against the true God. That's the sadness of it; that's what breaks my heart. The perfectionist is not against the gracious, loving, self-giving God who has come to us, who in Jesus Christ went all the way to the cross at such cost. No, his resentment is against a caricature of a god who is never satisfied. A god whom he can never please no matter how hard he tries, no matter what he gives up or holds on to. This cruel god always ups the ante a little, always demands a bit more and says, "Sorry, that wasn't quite good enough."

PERSONAL
REFLECTION

■ Before you write-off this "caricature-of-a-god-who-is-never-satisfied" idea and say that that type of thinking doesn't apply to you, I challenge you to take a deeper look inside. Rigid religious/Christian systems almost always bring us to that kind of subconscious conclusion. Take a moment right now to ask God to show you what, if any, distorted ideas you have of Him. Jot down any thoughts that come to mind.

_____

_____

_____

_____

Anger against this kind of god seethes up in the perfectionist. Sometimes his anger is recognized and the whole wretched ought-tyranny is seen for what it is: a desperate satanic substitute for true Christian perfection. And sometimes the perfectionist can work through all this, find grace, and marvelously be set free.

6. *Denial.* But too often the anger is not faced but denied. Because anger is considered a terrible sin, it is pushed down. And the whole mixture of bad theology, legalism, and salvation by performance becomes a frozen Niagara. This is when deep emotional problems set in. Mood changes are so great and so terrible that such a person seems to be two different people at the same time.

Under the stress and the strain of trying to live with a self he can't like, a God he can't love, and other people he can't get along with, the strain can become too much. And one of two things can happen: either there is a breakaway or a breakdown.

The *breakaway* is so sad. Much of my time is spent in counseling people who used to be active Christians but who have now broken away. The breakaway just throws the whole thing over. He doesn't become an unbeliever. He believes with his head but he can't believe with his heart. Perfectionism is impossible to live up to. He tried so many times and it made him so miserable that he just left it behind.

Others suffer a *breakdown.* The load is too heavy to bear, and they break under the weight. That's exactly what happened to Dr. Joseph R. Cooke, professor of anthropology at the University of Washington in Seattle. A brilliant Ph.D. and well trained in biblical theology, he became a missionary teacher to Thailand. But after a few years he left the mission field a broken man. A nervous breakdown left him no longer able to preach or teach or even to read his Bible. And as he put it, "I was a burden to my wife and useless to God and to others" (*Free for the Taking*, Fleming Revell, 1975).

How did this happen? "I invented an impossible God, and I had a nervous breakdown." Oh, he believed in grace, he even taught it. But his real feelings about the god he lived with day by day didn't correspond with his teaching. His god was ungracious and unpleasable.

God's demands of me were so high, and His opinion of me was so low, there was no way for me to live except under His frown. . . . All day long He nagged me: "Why don't you pray more? Why don't you witness more? When will you ever learn self-discipline? How can you allow yourself to indulge in such wicked thoughts? Do this. Don't do that. Yield, confess, work harder." . . . God was always using His love against me. He'd show me His nail-pierced hands, and then He would look at me glaringly and say, "Well, why aren't you a better Christian? Get busy and live the way you ought to."

Most of all, I had a God who down underneath considered me to be less than dirt. Oh, He made a great ado about loving me, but I believed that the day-to-day love and acceptance I longed for could only be mine if I let Him crush nearly everything that was really me. When I came down to it, there was scarcely a word or a feeling or a thought or a decision of mine that God really liked.

Can you understand why a sincere Christian who feels this way would have a total breakdown? And my years of preaching and counseling and praying with evangelical Christians lead me to believe that this disease of perfectionism is very common among church people.

PERSONAL REFLECTION

■ In what ways, if any, do you identify with the painful truth of Dr. Cooke's experience of God? Journal your thoughts and feelings about his experience.

_____

_____

_____

_____

There is only one ultimate cure for perfectionism; it is as profound and yet as simple as the word *grace*. Grace is simply our anglicized form of the Greek word *charis* which means "gracefulness, graciousness, kindness, a favor." But in the New Testament this word has a special meaning: "freely given, undeserved, unmerited, unearnable, and unrepayable favor." God's loving acceptance of us has nothing to do with our worthiness. As Dr. Cooke reminds us, grace is the face God wears when He meets our imperfection, sin, weakness, and failure. Grace is what God is and what God does when He meets the sinful and undeserving. Grace is a pure gift, free for the taking. The healing of perfectionism does not begin with some initial experience of grace in salvation or sanctification, and then move into a life lived by effort and perfect performance. The healing of perfectionism takes place in day-by-day believing, living, and realizing this grace relationship with a loving, caring Heavenly Father.

But that's the rub, for sometimes this cannot happen by itself. The realization of grace cannot be maintained in some people without a deep, inner reprogramming of all the bad conditioning that has been put into them by parents and family and teachers and preachers and the church.

These perfectionists have been programmed to unrealistic expectations, impossible performance, conditional love, and a subtle theology of works. They can't get rid of this pattern overnight. The change requires time, process, understanding, healing, and above all, reprogramming—the renewal of the mind that brings transformation.

I want to tell you how it happened in one young man's life. Don was raised in a strict evangelical home, where everything they believed in their heads was right, but where everything they practiced in everyday interpersonal relationships was wrong. Is that possible? Oh, yes! Very possible. And parents need to remember that it is not only what is taught to a child that matters, but also what is caught. Don was taught one thing, but he caught an opposite message, and was thus in great conflict.

Don grew up with unpredictable and conditional love. From his earliest childhood he was given to understand: "You will be loved IF . . ." "We will accept and approve you WHEN . . ." "You will be loved BECAUSE OF . . . IF YOU . . ." He grew up feeling that he never pleased his parents.

Don came to see me as a young adult in his thirties because his depressions were becoming more frequent, lasting longer, and were more frightening. Some well-meaning Christian friends told him that his problem was entirely spiritual. "Truly Spirit-filled Christians shouldn't have such feelings. They should always feel joyful." This left Don with a double burden: his problem, and his guilt because he had the problem.

Don and I spent many hours together. It wasn't easy for him to understand and accept God's love and grace, let alone to feel it at the gut level. Because every experience of interpersonal relationships from childhood to adulthood contradicted grace and love, it was very difficult for him to believe and feel God's grace.

And Don had added to his problem. During those down times he had entered into wrong relationships with the opposite sex. Oh, never all the way, but far enough that he would use this girl, and then that one, to help him pull out of his depression. That was sin and he knew it. Such misuse of another person added to his guilt, so that there was real guilt on top of his pseudoguilt. Again and again he had gone through the whole cycle of tears, repentance, salvation, and renewed promises, only to break them later.

Our process together took more than a year. But during this time there was healing of many painful memories and reprogramming of wrong ways of coping. He did his homework well, kept an honest journal of his feelings, read good books and listened to tapes, memorized many Scripture passages, and spent time in specific and positive prayer.

Some of the relearning took place in our relationship. He tried many, many times to maneuver me into rejecting him, and withdrawing my loving acceptance of him. Don was trying to get me to behave the way his mom and dad did and the way he thought God did.

Healing didn't happen overnight, but thank God, it happened! Slowly, but surely, Don discovered grace in God's incredible and unconditional acceptance of him as a person. His down times began to come less frequently. He didn't work at getting rid of them, they just left—like dead leaves fall off the tree in the springtime when the new leaves come. He gained more control over his thoughts and his actions. His depressions began to lift, until now he has the normal ups and downs that we all have.

Whenever I see Don alone he smiles and says, "Doc, it's still too good to be true, but it's true!" That's the message. The trouble with the perfectionist is that he has been programmed to think it is too good to be true. You too may think: *Of course, I believe in grace, but. . . .*

PERSONAL REFLECTION

■ In what ways do you relate with Don's story? Is it difficult for you to believe that God loves and accepts you unconditionally? Are you able to *feel* God's grace in your life? Write a little bit about your own spiritual journey to this point.

_____

_____

_____

"Come unto Me," said Jesus, "all ye that labor and are heavy laden, and I will give you rest" (Matt. 11:28). Isn't that good news? You don't have to live the way you do, for there's a better way to live! "I will give you rest. Take *My* yoke upon you . . . for My yoke is easy, and My burden is light" (vv. 28-30).

"My yoke is easy." What does that mean? His yoke is comfortable, because it is tailor-made to your personality, your individuality, and your humanity. "My burden is light," means that the Christ who fits you with a yoke will never leave you alone, but will always be yoked with you in the form of the Paraclete, the One who comes alongside to help you carry that comfortable burden and yoke.

Notice the words of Charles Wesley's hymn as he traced the progression of God's healing grace in a guilt-ridden, perfectionist's heart.

Arise, My Soul, Arise

Arise, my soul, arise; shake off thy guilty fears;
The bleeding Sacrifice in my behalf appears:
Before the throne my surety stands, before the throne my
    surety stands,
My name is written on His hands.

He ever lives above, for me to intercede;
His all-redeeming love, His precious blood, to plead:
His blood atoned for all our race, His blood atoned for
    all our race,
And sprinkles now the throne of grace.

Five bleeding wounds he bears, received on Calvary;
They pour effectual prayers; they strongly plead for me:
"Forgive him, O forgive," they cry, "forgive him,
    O forgive," they cry,
"Nor let that ransomed sinner die!"

The Father hears Him pray, His dear anointed One;
He cannot turn away the presence of His Son:
His Spirit answers to the blood, His Spirit answers to the
    blood,
And tells me I am born of God.

My God is reconciled; His pardoning voice I hear;
He owns me for His child; I can no longer fear:
With confidence I now draw nigh, with confidence I now
   draw nigh,
And "Father, Abba, Father," cry.

PRAYERFUL REFLECTION

■ The healing of perfectionism takes place on a day-to-day basis as we realize and *accept* God's grace (His freely given, unearnable kindness and favor) in our lives. Are you ready to receive God's perfect gift of grace? If so, hold out your hands like a child would to a loving parent and symbolically receive that gift. (If it feels comfortable, physically gesture using the hand motion described in the previous sentence.) Then, write a prayer, thanking God for His gift of grace. Tell Him whatever you need to about your fears or lack of feelings about Him. He understands. He longs for you to know Him more personally, more intimately. He's waiting for you to come to Him . . . to relieve you of any spiritual yokes you may be carrying . . . and give you rest.

_____

_____

_____

_____

_____

PERSONAL RENEWAL

■ Renew your thoughts and feelings this week by memorizing Matthew 11:28-30, (NIV). Jesus says:

> *"Come to Me, all you who are weary and burdened, and I will give you rest. Take My yoke upon you and learn from Me, for I am gentle and humble in heart, and you will find rest for your souls. For My yoke is easy and My burden is light."*

Surely He took up our infirmities and carried our sorrows, yet we considered Him stricken by God, smitten by Him, and afflicted. But He was pierced for our transgressions, He was crushed for our iniquities; the punishment that brought us peace was upon Him, and by His wounds we are healed. We all, like sheep, have gone astray, each of us has turned to his own way; and the Lord has laid on Him the iniquity of us all. . . . Therefore I will give Him a portion among the great, and He will divide the spoils with the strong, because He poured out His life unto death, and was numbered with the transgressors. For He bore the sin of many, and made intercession for the transgressors.

Isaiah 53:4-6, 12, NIV

Chapter 8
The Process of Healing for Perfectionism

Perfectionism is a constant and all-pervading feeling of never quite measuring up, never quite being or doing enough to please. To please whom? Everyone—yourself, others, and God. Naturally, a lot of self-belittling and self-contempt goes along with it, together with a supersensitivity to the opinions, to the approval, and the disapproval of others. And all of this is accompanied by a cloud of guilt. The perfectionist almost *has* to feel guilty, if for nothing else, not feeling guilty about something!

Perfectionism produces a distorted picture of God with feelings of doubt, rebellion, and anger against a God you can never please.

There is a cure for perfectionism in the graciousness of God who comes to us in Jesus Christ. But to experience this cure you need to accept the prescription for the process of healing.

The first step is to abandon all ideas of a quick cure. Don't let anyone delude you with the idea that a crisis cure will instantaneously heal you. In fact, part of the disease itself is to be always looking for a solution just around the corner. For perfectionism specializes in *if-onlys:* "If only I could _____

_____, I would be OK." How did you fill in the blank? With a *positive?* "If only I could . . . read, pray, give, witness, serve"? Or with a *negative?*

- "If only I could give up . . .
- "If only I could stop . . .
- "If only I could quit . . .
- "If only I could follow the four laws, or the three steps, or

receive the two blessings, or get the one gift; surely that would do it!"

Every such desperate grasp for quick solutions is a search for magic, not miracle. Healing is a process; you didn't get to be a perfectionist overnight, and you will not be healed overnight either. It will involve a process of growth in grace, of reprogramming, and of healing in every level of your life. You will need healing in your mind with its distorted concepts, healing of your feelings with their damaged emotions, healing of your perception with its downgrading evaluations, and healing of your relationships with all of their disruptive contradictions. You also need a deep inner healing of your memories to blot out the destructive, slow-motion video replays that interfere with the way you live.

You may think this sounds like a pretty thorough overhauling. It is, and your submission to this process is the beginning of healing for perfectionism.

PERSONAL REFLECTION

■ Emotional healing is a process. Your submission to this process is the beginning. Are you ready to begin? If so, read through the prayer which follows and sign your name in the blank at the end of the prayer, letting God know of your readiness.

> Lord Jesus,
> I believe that You have brought me to this place of
> healing in my life. I choose at this moment to trust
> You to complete the good work in me You have started.
> I understand that healing takes time; that there are no quick
> fixes. And I am committed to sticking with the process so
> that I find greater wholeness in my life. I ask You to:
>   √ Heal my mind of its distorted concepts;
>   √ Heal my feelings of their damaged emotions;
>   √ Heal my perception of its downgrading evaluations;
>   √ Heal my relationships of their disruptive contradictions;
>   √ Heal my memories of past hurts that replay in the present
> and interfere with the way I live.
>   I believe You will be with me in every step of the healing
> process and that You are enough to help me walk through the
> pain of it. Thank You for loving me enough to take me through
> the process of healing in my life.

_____

SIGN YOUR NAME HERE

Not only will God and His grace *be with you* in every step of the healing process, but God will *be pleased with you* at every step of the process. In the Bible the word *grace* is always woven into the presence of the Giver of grace. We should never use the word *grace* as if we were describing some kind of commodity that God dispenses. Grace means a gracious God coming to you. "My grace is sufficient" (2 Cor. 12:9). Not *grace* by "My grace." One of Paul's favorite phrases was "the grace of our Lord Jesus Christ" (1 Cor. 16:23; Gal. 6:18; Phil. 4:23; 1 Thes. 5:28; 2 Thes. 3:18). Grace is not a commodity but our Lord Himself, coming to us in His graciousness. A loving, gracious God accepts us as we are, offers Himself lovingly to us right here and now, not when we shape up.

God is as pleased with you when you are in this healing process as loving parents are when their child starts learning to walk. Those are exciting days in a home, especially with the first child—the child stumbles, knocks over the furniture, may even bend the lamp a bit. But do the parents scold him, tell him how displeased they are because he isn't doing a perfect job? Does Dad shout, "You ought to do better than that, kid"? Does Mother chime in with, "That sure was a stupid step you took. No wonder you fell and hurt yourself"? Do you see how we often have made God into a neurotic parent? If Jesus were preaching His Sermon on the Mount, He might paraphrase this idea: "If you being evil know how to do that well when teaching your child to walk, how much more will the Heavenly Father be pleased with every step in your healing process." (See Matt. 7:11.) God will be pleased with you, every step of the way.

Let me suggest a prayer to go along with this, a prescription, to take as often as needed. **"Thank You, Lord, that You are healing me according to Your perfect schedule."** In this way you turn the process not into another form of irritation for your perfectionism, or anger at your slow progress, but into a prayer of thanksgiving for His graciousness every step of the way.

PERSONAL REFLECTION

■ Your healing process may have begun before you started working through this book. Or you may just now be starting on your journey toward healing. No matter where you are in the process, this is the truth—God is *pleased* with you every step of the way. How does it make you feel, knowing God is pleased with you?

_____

_____

_____

_____

_____

Emotional problems often result from the kind of a god, the kind of people, the kind of life we saw, as we looked through the relational windows of our childhood. Most of us developed our concept/feelings about our Heavenly Father from our earthly mothers and fathers, and these feelings become intertwined and confused. But the guilty and contradictory feelings are not the voice of God. They are often the continuing voice of Mother or Dad or Brother or Sister, or something internalized that puts pressure on us. Remember, most of our basic patterns for relating to other people come from the patterns of the relationships of our family.

1. Unpleaseable parents. One of the most common parental family situations which produces perfectionism and depression is unpleaseable parents. Such parents give only conditional love which demands that certain standards are lived up to, top grades achieved, or the highest kind of performance met in athletics or in spiritual life. There is little or no affirmation and plenty of criticism. Even approval is conditional. Encouragement is given but only to stress the fact the "you should have and could have done better." The three A's on the report card aren't mentioned, but the B—"I think you can pull the B up to an A if you try harder." And then when you do try harder and you get that B pulled up to an A and you show the report card to Mother, sure she is going to be pleased, she looks at you for a moment and all of a sudden frowns and says, "My goodness! Where did you get that stain on your jacket! You must have spilled catsup on yourself at the cafeteria. Have you been going around all day looking like that!" Which really translated means, "You lousy ungrateful kid. What kind of a parent are you making me look like before the community?"

Unpleaseable parents and conditional love produce unreachable goals and unattainable standards. Some years ago a lady told me that every time I used the word *obey* or *obedience* in a sermon, she would feel uneasy and guilty. Her mother used to dress her up in the morning for play, in very fancy clothing. And then she would say, "Now, when you go out, don't get any dirt on that pretty dress of yours. I worked hard to iron all those ruffles." You can well imagine what the dress looked like by afternoon and evening. And when the little girl came in, her mother would scold her angrily: "You naughty girl, you never obey me." Absurd, unrealistic, unattainable demands were made. And when they weren't achieved, guilt and punishment were meted out. Since this was a deeply religious home, are you surprised that the child, now a grown woman, struggles with wretched concepts of God, with low self-esteem, and a cloud of guilt?

PERSONAL REFLECTION

■ In his book, *Love: No Strings Attached* (Nelson, 1987), Rich Buhler expresses the idea that we often confuse love and approval. *Approval* must be earned and is granted because of what a person does. Approval has to do with "doing." Approval can be lost.

Describe a time when you lost the approval of someone who was important to you. How did you feel in relationship to that person?

_____

_____

_____

_____

_____

■ Love is anything that is done for a person because of what that person is. There are no strings attached to unconditional love. Give an example from your life of being *conditionally* loved. What did it cost you to get that love? Then cite an example of someone loving you *unconditionally*.

_____

_____

_____

_____

_____

■ In what ways are you still trying to gain the approval and love of your parents? Are you doing it through overachievement? Avoiding conflict? Being a people-pleaser? What keeps you stuck in this pattern of relating to your parents?

_____

_____

_____

_____

2. *Unpredictable home situations.* In one of his works, Charles Dickens said, "In the world of little children, the greatest hurt of all is

injustice." Unpredictable home situations produce injustice. If parents cannot control their own emotions, a child never knows what kind of response he is going to get from them.

Beth had a terribly up-and-down Christian life. She tried hard, but faith and even trust were so difficult. Her feelings of condemnation and guilt were so strong at times that she couldn't bear to come to church. Finally, we made a deal—she would sit way back, close to one of the exits, so that if she couldn't bear something from my sermon, she could walk out. And many, many times in the midst of a sermon when I wasn't talking about anything that *I* thought was heavy, I would see Beth get up and walk out.

What a home she had! It was like living on eggshells day and night. Her father was an alcoholic. Her mother was one of those quiet, gentle people—quiet and gentle like a dormant volcano which can erupt at any time. I'll never forget Beth's statement: "I never knew if I would get hugged or slugged. And I could never figure out the reason for either one." So, of course, she thought God was as unpredictable, irrational, and unreliable as her parents were.

Besides those emotional scars, there were some literal scars. Surgery once was required on a dislocated jaw. And those scars had left deeply painful memories which needed healing before she could believe in the God from whom every good and perfect gift comes, the God in whom there is light without the slightest shadow of variation or change (James 1:17).

It's not hard to see how such home situations are the breeding grounds for emotional cripples and perfectionists. Unpleaseable parents, unacceptable selfhood, unrealistic, unattainable standards, unclear signals, unendurable conflicts—all program people to the wrong kind of responses.

PERSONAL REFLECTION

■ Would you describe the home where you grew up as "unpredictable"? Give a few examples that show the unpredictability of that home.

_____

_____

_____

_____

_____

■ For a child, growing up in an unpredictable home is very painful. A child senses the injustice of this type of environment, and feels hurt because of it. He or she may be unable to express those feelings of hurt. Consequently, when the pain of the hurt gets too great, a child most often will bury those feelings. Those feelings stay buried or frozen, and often, it isn't until adulthood that the feelings begin to emerge. Adult children have difficulty identifying their feelings because they are so deeply buried. We all have many feelings; some we are willing to expose to others, others we choose to keep hidden. From the list below, identify the feelings you are willing to expose to others. Then identify the feelings you choose to keep hidden.

Feelings

love	anger	loneliness	confusion
hurt	guilt	shyness	embarrassment
fear	caring	jealousy	understanding
worry	warmth	patience	excitement
hate	sadness	sympathy	moodiness
shame	gloom	discouragement	encouragement

FEELINGS I CAN EXPRESS   **FEELINGS I KEEP HIDDEN**

_____   _____

_____   _____

_____   _____

_____   _____

_____   _____

_____   _____

_____   _____

Do you understand why healing is a process that needs time, effort, ofttimes the help of a counselor, and always the supportive, loving fellowship of the body of Christ? How we need the affirmation, the support, and the ministry from fellow members of the body of Christ! James implies that in many cases the reprogramming, renewing, and healing process comes about only as we share with and pray for one another (James 5:16).

Countless hurts that come to us are hard to classify. They are part and parcel of living in a fallen world. Ben was one of the most timid souls I have ever counseled. I couldn't even hear him. "What did you say, Ben?" We began practicing to raise Ben's voice. I would have him read things to me. "A little louder, Ben. Assert yourself. Speak up!" He was so afraid to be a burden to people. It could make a person uncomfortable to be around him. You might look to see if he was wearing a sandwich board that read, "Excuse me for living."

Have you ever heard of the "Dependent Order of Really Meek and Timid Souls"? When you make an acrostic of its first letters, you have "Doormats." The Doormats have an official insignia—a yellow caution light. Their official motto is: "The meek shall inherit the earth, if that's OK with everybody!" The society was founded by Upton Dickson who wrote a pamphlet called "Cower Power." Well, Ben could have been a charter member of the Doormats.

Improvement for Ben began in the process of talking things over, but the real healing opened up at a marriage enrichment weekend. Surrounded by a loving, accepting, affirming group of couples, Ben began to recall a series of painful memories. He remembered hearing the neighbors talk about his family. You see, his mother was a frail, hysterical woman. She'd had a nervous breakdown and had spent many years as a semi-invalid. And he remembered the neighbors whispering that she had had the breakdown because her little boy just followed her around, clinging to her apron strings, and never letting her out of his sight. A pretty heavy burden to lay on a toddler or even on a teenager—"*You* are the cause of your mother's breakdown, of her being an invalid." Now Ben sobbed with release, and how beautifully the group loved and accepted him. There was lifted from him a great burden, for he could stop the inner penance he had done all those years for an unjust accusation.

How much hurt and damage have been done from chance remarks like this one we'll never know. Seeds of hurt, humiliation, and hate are sown into a little mind, to fester, to become gangrenous, and someday to infect an adult personality.

Remarks like this one: "I'm afraid he'll grow up to be just like his Uncle Ed." And who is Uncle Ed? Well, Uncle Ed just happened to have spent ten years in the pen; he died in a mental institution.

Or this one: "Boy, that kid, that face. Isn't it a shame he couldn't have gotten just a little bit of his brother's good looks?"

Or the little girl, with the most beautiful sister, who overheard the relatives whispering at the family reunion, "That's the homely one."

PERSONAL REFLECTION

■ Words that wound . . . we all have them. What are some of the wounding words other people said to you as a child? As a teenager? As an adult? Like Ben in the previous story, your expressing or writing down those wounding words will begin to take some of the sting out of them. Tackle this exercise as fearlessly as you can.

_____

_____

_____

_____

_____

_____

■ In what ways are "wounding words" from the past impairing your life in the present?

_____

_____

_____

_____

_____

_____

And what can we possibly say about all the hurts and agonies, the guilts and fears and the hates that are intertwined with the American obsession—sex? All the way from those childish curiosities where children explore each other's bodies, to older brothers and sisters with threats or bribes taking advantage of younger ones, arousing powerful feelings—that are destructive at that age—like running 800 volts through 110 wire. Move on to fathers and stepfathers who treat their daughters not as daughters, but as wives and mistresses. Sex, being what it is, can produce the deadliest of all emotional conflicts: dread and desire, fear and pleasure, love and hate, all combined into a violent emotional earthquake which can tear a person's guts out.

PERSONAL REFLECTION

■ According to a 1985 study on "Domestic Violence" done by *Instructional Aides, Inc.*, 1 out of 3–4 girls and 1 out of 5–8 boys experience some form of sexual abuse. Perhaps that was your experience as a child. If so, it is very painful to look at. God wants to bring healing to this wounded area of your life. If you were sexually abused, write a few sentences expressing to God the emotional conflicts you've agonized over as the result of that abuse.

_____

_____

_____

_____

_____

Speaking of hate—that's the real problem, isn't it? The anger, the resentment, the hate that gets buried deep down inside. Sometimes I ask people when I'm counseling with them, "Would the word *rage* be too strong?" They often hang their heads and say, "No. That's right." Don't let an external doormat meekness fool you. I have yet to deal with a person troubled by perfectionistic emotional problems who was not very angry about something. The anger may be buried underneath layers of timidity, meekness, and spiritual piety, but it's there.

The healing process must include the courage to unmask the anger, bring it out before God, and put it on the cross where it belongs. There will be no healing until it is acknowledged, confronted, and resolved. Resolution means forgiving every person involved in that hurt and humiliation; it means surrendering every desire for a vindictive triumph over that person; it means allowing God's forgiving love to wash over your guilt-plagued soul.

I was surprised to get a phone call many years ago from a professor in a Christian college. He remembered a statement I had made, while preaching a revival at his school. He said, "I remember you saying, 'Whenever you experience a response on your part that is way out of proportion to the stimulus, then look out. You have probably tapped into some deeply hidden emotional hurt.' I guess that is what has happened to me." So he came to our town, and we spent almost a week together. He was a learned man, and highly spiritual, with a deep knowledge of Scripture. But there had been a confrontation on that college campus, and all of a sudden this controlled, Christian scholar was reacting in violent anger. *Rage* was really the word for it. He was shocked at himself, and felt so guilty. He didn't know what to do, and no amount of Scripture reading or praying or trying to leave the whole situation with God seemed to help. He was really on the brink and in agony confessed to me: "I can't believe it, but when this happened, I actually felt as if I wanted to go out and kill somebody."

It wasn't hard to find the roots of the problem, but he had trouble accepting them. As he told me about it he kept saying, "Oh, but that's so silly . . . it can't be that!"

I said, "Nothing is silly. Tell me about it."

He had been a bright, precocious child, an egghead almost from birth. You know the kind—six years old, going on fifteen. He was so bright that it wasn't easy for him to live with the ones who weren't as smart. He was always first in the classroom but last on the playground. Every recess was a hell for him. There were those unforgettable scenes, as the intelligent but uncoordinated little boy was teased and made fun of. The rougher and tougher boys and girls bullied him, tortured him, knocked him down, hurt him physically. But more than that, they made an emotional cripple out of him. He was amazed at the sensitivity of his memory. He remembered all the children by name, and even what they wore. It was all there, though years had elapsed, and he tapped into this fountain of rage. As we went through every incident, he called each youngster by name. We put every one under his forgiveness. "Will you forgive Dan? Will you forgive Sally? And will you forgive . . ." Does this sound trivial? Quite the contrary, it was incredibly painful. But in prayer he found grace to forgive each one of those kids who had made life so intolerable for him. The Holy Spirit took the sting out of those memories and defused their compulsive power. That was the beginning of an in-depth change, and it took time until the healing power of God filled in those torturous, hurtful holes in his heart.

PERSONAL REFLECTION

■ Unmasking hidden anger is not any easy thing to do. There are reasons for your anger—the many things that were said, things that happened, words that were never said that you needed to hear. Yet in learning to survive, much of that anger was never expressed—it was denied, minimized, and discounted. Complete the following sentences:

When I was a child, I remember being angry about _____

_____

_____

When I was a teenager, I remember being angry about _____

_____

_____

As an adult, I get angry when_____

_____

_____

NOTE: *If you have difficulty identifying your anger, you may want to think in terms of the words* **frustrated, disgusted, irritated, upset about.**

■ Describe how you dealt with your anger as a child. How did your mother respond when you expressed anger? What was your father's response to anger? How did your mother and father handle their own anger?

_____

_____

_____

_____

■ Perfectionists often have a hard time dealing with their anger. Many times they are not aware of it. Or they may be so afraid of their own anger or frightened by another person's anger that they are paralyzed by it. Is it difficult for you to express your anger? Find out by completing the following sentences:

When I am angry, I_____

_____

When I am angry, I feel _____

_____

If other people saw me angry, I'd_____

_____

When other people get angry, I _____

_____

Such basic inner resentment is really an anger against injustice and it cries out, "I was a victim. I had no choice. I didn't choose to be born. I didn't choose my parents. I didn't choose my brothers and sisters. I didn't choose my handicaps and my illness. I was a victim, and my hurts and my humiliations and my scars are unjust." And we often see this hidden anger coming out in perfectionists who want to correct every mistake they see and set right all the wrongs of the world.

PERSONAL REFLECTION

■ Do you find yourself unusually sensitive to "unjust situations" in your work setting, in other people's relationships, in your own relationships, in politics and government? Cite a few examples of injustices you've tried to correct. How did you try to bring about justice in each situation?

_____

_____

_____

_____

_____

_____

_____

The place of healing for this damaged person is the cross—the very peak of all injustice. In P.T. Forsythe's profound book, he calls the cross "the justification of God" (_The Justification of God_, London, Independent Press). In the cross God demonstrated His total identification with us in _our undeserved suffering,_ as well as in _our deserved punishment._ Never was there more injustice than in that cross. No one ever received more rejection than our Lord. His accusations, His trial, His crucifixion were all vastly unjust.

Never say, "God doesn't know what it is like to suffer" and never think that God allows us to suffer things that He has not been willing to bear Himself. He was led as a Lamb to the slaughter; all His rights were taken from Him; all His powers were suspended. The support of His friends was removed, as they forsook Him and fled, while He was humiliated, stripped, mocked, ridiculed. "So you're the Son of God, huh? Well, come down and prove it if You are so great."

As we look at the cross, we begin to see how deeply Christ is the _truth,_ and not just the bright, shiny, beautiful truth of God _for_ all of us. His cross is the ghastly, revolting truth *about* all of us—the truth about the envy and the hate and the lust and the selfishness and the rage that permeate this fallen, sinful world of human beings. The truth of life in this world came out in the crucifixion of the Son of God. Now we know that God understands what it is like to live in this kind of a world. He is the Wounded Healer, He is our High Priest who is touched with the feelings of our infirmities.

Here is the unbelievable, too-good-to-be-true good news for every perfectionist—for you who cannot face all those conflicting feelings inside you which you think you can't possibly share with God. I've heard a thousand times in my office, "How can I tell these things to God? How can I express my hurt, my humiliation, my anger, my resentment against people; yes, against Him? How can I share *that* with Him?" Don't you understand? On the cross He has already experienced all of that and far more.

On the cross, God in Christ has absorbed all these kinds of painful feelings into His love. They have entered into His heart, pierced His soul, and been dissolved in the ocean of His forgiveness and the sea of His forgetfulness.

The Apostle Paul, formerly the bitterest enemy of the Christian faith, was the one who hated Jesus Christ, the one who hurled insults at Him, the one who vented his rage by being at the killing of the first martyr, Stephen. When Paul discovered that all that rage had been absorbed into the gracious heart of God, he wrote, "God was in Christ, reconciling [let's make it personal], reconciling *me* to Himself, not counting *my* trespasses against me." (See 2 Cor. 5:19.)

There is *nothing* you an share out of the agonizing hurts and depths and hates and rages of your soul that God has not heard. There is *nothing* you take to Him that He will not understand. He will receive you with love and grace.

Because Jesus knew that we would all think this was too good to be true, on the night before He went to the cross, He instituted the Communion Supper. Taking bread and wine, simple things we could feel and touch and taste and smell and receive into ourselves, He said, "Eat and drink this to remind you of it all." (See Matt. 26:26-28.)

As we take and eat of the body, from His brokenness we receive healing and wholeness for our brokenness. As we partake of the cup, we receive His forgiving and healing love into our souls and bodies.

"O Wounded Healer, Broken One, we give You all the broken pieces of our lives, and ask that You put them all together and make us whole. Amen."

PERSONAL REFLECTION

■ Dr. Seamands states, "There is *nothing* you can share out of the agonizing hurts and depths and hates and rages of your soul that God has not heard. There is *nothing* you take to Him that He will not understand. He will receive you with love and grace." Do you believe that with all your heart? Why or why not?

_____

_____

_____

_____

■ In Alcoholics Anonymous there is a familiar saying: "You're only as sick as your secrets." In the deepest part of our souls lie the ugliest acts of our humanity—the things we don't want anyone to know about us because there is so much shame attached to them. The good news is . . . on the cross, God in Christ came to pay for those shameful acts. Through Christ we can receive *full pardon* for the wrongs we have done and be set free from the hurtful things that have been done to us. The first step is to acknowledge our "secrets" to God. We can find forgiveness and restoration at the cross. What shameful deeds of your life (things you may never have told anyone) need to be brought to the cross today? Write them down.

_____

_____

_____

_____

PRAYERFUL REFLECTION

■ In the cross God demonstrated His total identification with us in *our undeserved suffering*, as well as in *our deserved punishment*. He was led as a Lamb to the slaughter; all His rights were taken from Him; His powers were suspended; His friends and family abandoned Him; He was humiliated, mocked, and ridiculed. In what ways have you experienced these kinds of things in your life? Though He lived a perfect life, Christ chose to die for the wrongs we have done. He paid the price—His life—so we wouldn't have to pay. How does that make you feel? Answer the key questions in this paragraph in the form of a prayer.

O Wounded Healer, Broken One,

Thank You for _____

_____

_____

_____

_____

_____

_____

_____

_____

PERSONAL RENEWAL

■ Seven hundred years before the birth of Christ, the Prophet Isaiah told of the Suffering Servant who would come. This prophetic description of Jesus Christ is a beautiful reminder of God's incredible identification with us as wounded people. Draw comfort from Isaiah's words this week as you meditate on Isaiah 53:2-7, 11-12 (NCV).

> He grew up like a small plant before the Lord. He was like a root growing in a dry land. He had no special beauty or form to make us notice Him. There was nothing in His appearance to make us desire Him. But He took our suffering on Him and felt our pain for us. We saw His suffering. We thought God was punishing Him. But He was wounded for the wrong things we did. He was crushed for the evil things we did. The punishment, which made us well, was given to Him. And we are healed because of His wounds. We all have wandered away like sheep. Each of us has gone his own way. But the Lord has put on Him the punishment for all the evil we have done. He was beaten down and punished.
> But He didn't say a word. He was like a lamb being led to be killed. He was quiet, as a sheep is quiet while its wool is being cut. He never opened His mouth. . . . He will suffer many things in His soul. But then He will see life and be

satisfied. My Good Servant will make many people right with God. He carried away their sins. For this reason I will make Him a great man among people. He will share in all things with those who are strong. He willingly gave His life. He was treated like a criminal. But He carried away the sins of many people. And He asked forgiveness for those who sinned.

We do not dare to classify or compare ourselves with some who commend themselves. When they measure themselves by themselves and compare themselves with themselves, they are not wise. We however, will not boast beyond proper limits, but will confine our boasting to the field God has assigned to us, a field that reaches even to you. . . .

But, "Let him who boasts boast in the Lord." For it is not the one who commends himself who is approved, but the one whom the Lord commends.

2 Corinthians 10:12-13, 17-18, NIV

Surely You desire truth in the inner parts; You teach me wisdom in the inmost place.

Psalm 51:6, NIV

Chapter 9
Super You or Real You?

The perfectionist needs to learn to be his true self in Christ. Yet it's in being his real self that the perfectionist runs into his biggest snags, and needs his deepest healing and most drastic reprogramming. Perhaps the most terrible consequence of perfectionism is alienation from the true self. Let's see where this tragic loss begins and how it takes place.

Somewhere in the process of growing up, the child receives messages about himself, about God, and about other people, and about relationships. These messages can be taught or caught. They can come through what is directly said or done, or what is *not* said and *not* done. Usually it is a combination of many factors. Slowly but surely, and quite unconsciously to the youngster, the messages come through. The child who has received negative messages then knows: "I am not accepted and loved as I am. I've tried every way to get this approval by being the way I am. Now I can only be accepted and loved *if* I become something else and someone else."

This youngster doesn't sit down and figure this all out. He doesn't know what is happening in his life—that he is not receiving fulfillment of deep, God-given needs which are basic to the development of a human being. Some very necessary feelings never come across to him, feelings like security, acceptance, belongingness, and value. His need to be loved and to learn to give love is not met. Instead there develops a growing deep anxiety, and feelings of insecurity, unworthiness, and undesirableness. And the youngster begins to climb the long, torturous trail of trying to become someone else.

PERSONAL REFLECTION

■ When you were a child, what kinds of messages did you receive about yourself, about God, about other people, and about relationships? Most likely you are still holding on to some, if not many, of those messages. *EXAMPLES: My value is in what I do. God can't use me unless I'm spiritually strong. Women are emotional and unstable. Men are logical and insensitive. I must have everyone's love and approval to be happy.* Try to identify some messages that were communicated to you in your home and write them down below.

Messages about Myself

_____

_____

_____

_____

Messages about God

_____

_____

_____

_____

Messages about Persons of the Opposite Sex

_____

_____

_____

_____

Messages about Persons of the Same Sex

_____

_____

_____

Messages about Relationships

_____

_____

_____

_____

The tragedy is that the person's God-designed selfhood doesn't ever get a chance to grow. His unique talents are not developed. His true self is denied or squelched, and a kind of pseudo-self takes its place. All the emotional and spiritual energies which ought to go into the development of his God-intended self are used to create a false and idealized picture of himself.

Unfortunately, when this person becomes a Christian, this self-destructive process is not automatically stopped. Forgiveness, loving acceptance, and God's grace penetrate some outer layers of his unreal self, bringing a new spirit of honesty to his life.

But if the distortion is serious and the emotions are badly damaged, a deeper kind of healing is needed. For all too often, the pseudo-self transfers over into the Christian life itself, and reorganizes around the new religious experience.

PERSONAL REFLECTION

■ The term "inner child" has become well known in recovery circles today. Dr. Richard Dickinson in his book, _The Child in Each of Us,_ describes the inner child as "that part of you that feels deeply, needs deeply, and loves deeply. Your inner child consists of your feelings, your natural talents, and your creativity—the unique dimensions of your personality." According to this definition, describe in two or three sentences what you know about your inner child.

_____

_____

_____

_____

_____

■ How "public" have you made your inner child? Do you feel like family, friends, and people you meet for the first time get a true picture of the real you? Explain.

_____

_____

_____

_____

_____

What are *Super You* and *Real You?* Super You is a false idealized image you think you have to be in order to be loved and accepted. Super You is an imaginary picture of yourself. Since you have been programmed to believe that no one will love you if he gets to know the real you, you strive to become Super You, to gain love and acceptance.

PERSONAL REFLECTION

■ In what ways have you changed your outer self (the way you look, act, think, and feel) in order to gain other people's love and acceptance? Exercise a lot of self-honesty in answering this question.

_____

_____

_____

_____

_____

This distortion extends even to God who is Absolute Perfection, who demands perfection, and to whom you must somehow present only your good side. You must let God see only Super You, not Real You.

Let me ask you a very personal question. When you come into the presence of God in meditation or prayer, which of the two do you present to Him? I asked that once of a successful evangelist who had come seeking help for some emotional and spiritual problems. I said to him, "In your dealings with God, when you go to Him in prayer, which self do you present to Him? What's the picture of yourself, in your imagination, that you are bringing to God?" I said, "Don't answer quickly. Take your time. We'll just sit and you think about it."

Well, he was silent for an unusually long time. Then he said to me, "You know, I've never really thought of it that way before. But I've got to be honest with you. I'm afraid that I always go into the presence of God with my best spiritual foot forward and my finest halo on. I would have to, in honesty, admit that when I imagine myself in the presence of God, I'm always Super Me. I don't think I have ever gone as Real Me, just as I am." And then he shook his head and said, "And I've sung that song a thousand times, 'Just As I Am,' but I have never lived it out when I came to God."

PERSONAL REFLECTION

■ Which self do you present to God—your Super Self or your Real Self? Briefly describe the self you present in your dealings with God.

_____

_____

_____

_____

_____

There are subtle ways of presenting Super Self to God and hiding Real Self. One is the *futuristic* way. "Well, God, of course, I haven't achieved Super Me yet. You know that and I know that. I'm not the picture of Super Me yet, but someday I will be. Someday I'm going to be that perfect Christian. Someday I'll pray enough, read enough, witness enough, do enough sensational things for You. Someday I will be the idealized picture of myself. I'll be Super Me. So don't pay attention to Real Me now, God—that's just temporary. Get Your eyes on what I am going to be."

Then there's the *penitential* way. And this is where so much low self-esteem and even self-contempt comes into the perfectionist's life. "Well, God, don't look at Real Me, with all my sins and failures and my shortcomings. Don't look at that because You can see how much I despise Real Me, can't You? And I presume, of course, that You too hate Real Me with all my failures and shortcomings. But You know what my goals are, Lord. Since You hate Real Me and I hate Real Me, You can see I'm really on Your side, so I'm really Super Me."

In these subtle ways, self-belittling becomes a perpetual inner penance to impress God. You hope He doesn't see your Real Self, but only looks at your Super Self. Since God can't stand that ugly, unacceptable Real You and since you keep telling Him you can't stand it either, He must be impressed with your very high standards, realize what you really are, and therefore, accept and love you.

The tragedy of this is that Real You got stuck emotionally at some childhood level. And this explains some of the utterly childish things that come out of your personality. You stayed in the past somewhere; you never grew. You obviously have the chronological body of a man or a woman, but spiritually and emotionally you live on an immature level.

PERSONAL REFLECTION

■ In *When I Grow Up* . . . author Ron Ross writes, "At all stages, children must be loved, cared for, affirmed and guided in order to develop into mature adults. If we are abused or deprived of what we need as children, we age chronologically but do not mature emotionally. When we reach adulthood, we are actually children trapped in adult bodies. We are often referred to as adult children" (Recovery Publications, 1990, p. 41). Listed below are some common behaviors that characterize adult children's lives (*When I Grow Up* . . . p. 46). Which of these would you say are evident in your life? Check all that apply.

Common Behaviors of Adult Children

❑ We are incapable of building and maintaining enduring, meaningful, and intimate relationships with God, ourselves, or others.

❑ We find it difficult to trust ourselves or others in a deepening fashion; thus, it is hard for us to live by faith.

❑ We do not possess the skills or vocabulary necessary for the healthy communication of feelings, preferences, ideas, or needs.

❑ We do not know how to manage the inevitable stresses of life; we cannot easily play, relax, or rest.

❑ We do not possess the skills necessary to understand God's will in our lives.

❑ We are resistant to change.

❑ We are rigid and inflexible in our thoughts and actions.

❑ We lack the ability to grow spiritually and emotionally.

❑ We do not know how or where to seek help or to offer help to others.

❑ We do not know how to handle adult responsibilities and relationships.

❑ We often feel that we do not belong anywhere.

❑ We have difficulty developing healthy beliefs, morals, and values.

❑ We have a strong need to be in control.

❑ We have difficulty following projects through from beginning to end.

❑ We feel guilty when we stand up for ourselves.

❑ We give in to others instead of taking care of ourselves.

It is in the area of feelings that the perfectionist has his biggest problems, because the image of Super Self is a person who never admits to experiencing certain kinds of feelings. Usually he has an unbiblical mental picture of Jesus as "gentle Jesus, meek and mild." This Jesus is sissified, passive, a stoic person whose emotions are never expressed. He's under the tightest emotional control; and usually doesn't express emotions at all.

However, there are not such things as bad feelings and good feelings. Feelings just *are*. They are consequences of a whole range of things that come out of your personality. No emotions are in themselves sinful. What you do with them will determine whether they are wrong or right. How you handle them will determine whether they lead you to righteousness or to sinfulness. The emotions themselves are a very important part of your God-given personality equipment.

One emotion that Super You generally considers bad is *anger*. I grew up on some unbiblical, inhuman, and destructive preaching about anger always being an unsanctified emotion. It took me years to get over these attitudes. They almost destroyed my Christian life and nearly wrecked my marriage, because I had to learn how to properly express my anger to my wife. Every good husband or wife has to learn how to do that in acceptable ways.

In Mark 3:5 we read that Jesus looked around at them in anger. While this is the only place in the New Testament that actually says Jesus got angry, I think we can safely presume that Jesus was angry when He whipped the money changers out of the temple and when He called certain people "blind fools," "whitewashed tombs," "murderers," "serpents," and "miserable frauds." (See Matt. 23, PH.) Never was Jesus more divine than at those moments when He was expressing white-hot anger. Many times, perfect love and anger go hand in hand; indeed, the anger is the result of perfect love.

We Christians have a semantic trick that sounds good but confuses people. "Oh, that's not anger; it's 'righteous indignation.'" Why don't we just come out and say that there is a right use of anger, and that anger in itself is not a sinful emotion? It would be a lot less confusing.

What matters is your use of anger—how you express it and how you resolve it. But when you have this unreal, false image of Super You who must never experience or never express any feelings of anger, you become a perfect setup for emotional wreckage and depression.

PERSONAL REFLECTION

■ Is it difficult for you to express certain emotions? Which ones? Why?

_____

_____

_____

_____

_____

■ Describe a time when you used anger in a constructive way. How did you express it and how did you resolve it?

_____

_____

_____

_____

Don't confuse anger and resentment, for they are entirely different. Anger, controlled and properly expressed, is one thing; out-of-control anger, improperly expressed, is another. The Apostle Paul made a plain distinction between the right kind of anger and resentment. He carefully contrasted anger with hate, malice, bitterness, and all the rest of it. Interestingly enough, his statement, "Be ye angry and sin not" (Eph. 4:26), is in the imperative. Paul didn't say, "It's all right, I will allow you to get angry once in a while as a concession." Paul said, "Get angry! Be angry!" He was quick to add, "But be careful." Paul knew that anger can lead to resentment, malice, bitterness, if it is not handled very carefully. Paul was saying, "Express your anger, but be sure that it doesn't lead you into any form of bitterness, resentment, or hatred." Now the strange fact of the matter is that unless you and I learn proper ways of expressing and resolving anger, we will become resentful and bitter. Many marriages are being destroyed because partners have not learned how to properly express their anger. They are keeping the lid on a lot of deep feelings, doing a slow burn, and getting even in a thousand and one subtle ways.

Be angry, but be careful. Anger becomes resentful and bitter when you don't know proper ways to express it. This is exactly what happens to the perfectionist who can never even allow himself to express anger; who won't even allow himself to be aware that he is angry. He denies it and pushes it down deep into his inner self where it simmers and festers and comes out in various kinds of disguised emotional problems, marital conflicts, and even in forms of physical illness.

Anger is a divinely implanted emotion, part of God's image in the human personality, and is to be used for constructive purposes.

PERSONAL REFLECTION

■ Dr. Seamands reminds us that "unless you and I learn proper ways of expressing and resolving anger, we will become resentful and bitter." Have you ever been resentful and bitter because of unexpressed or unresolved anger? When? Describe what happened to make you angry and why the situation was left unresolved.

_____

_____

_____

_____

_____

■ Think back to a time when you worked through an "angry" situation and brought it to a healthy resolution. How did you do it? Write down your process of resolution for future reference.

_____

_____

_____

_____

Super You has the notion that you ought to always get along with everybody, be liked by everybody, and that there should never be any conflict between Christians.

A brief visit to a mission station is a shock for the perfectionist, because it doesn't take him long to realize that the missionaries often have more problems in getting along with one another than with the other unbelievers they are trying to minister to. We see this in our own churches. But still the perfectionist myth persists: "This is what I ought to be."

Does such an idea come from Scripture? Not even two greats like Paul and Barnabas could work together. Very wisely they parted company, and very wisely the early church laid hands on them both, blessed them both, and sent them in opposite directions.

God used their humanness to establish two mission works instead of one. God also used their disagreement to help John Mark to mature and become the great writer of the Gospel of Mark.

While you cannot work with everybody, that doesn't mean you have the right to hate or to be bitter. It *does* mean you may not necessarily like or feel comfortable around everybody. And don't let Super You become your Screwtape who says, "Well now, if you're not getting along, *you* are the one at fault. The problem is *you*, and if only you would take care of something, you'd get along OK." Paul never said, "If you are filled with the Holy Spirit, you will live peacefully and smoothly with all people." What he did say is, "If possible, so far as it depends on you, be at peace with all men" (Rom. 12:18, NASB). The problem may lie in the other person. Paul did not add, as Super You does, "Yes, and that problem is also your problem and you are responsible for fixing the other guy up too." There is a little rhyme that says it well:

> To live above with saints in heaven,
> Oh, that will be glory;
> But to live below with saints on earth—
> Now that's a different story.

Real You faces real differences, real conflicts, and loves and cares enough to confront persons in a spirit of love. But Real You also knows that sometimes the best solution and the only solution is, to use Stanley Jones' great phrase, "to agree to disagree agreeably."

PERSONAL REFLECTION

■ Are you able to face your differences with other people and confront when necessary, or do you find it nearly impossible to confront someone? What kinds of people do you have difficulty confronting? Why do you think it is difficult for you to confront them?

_____

_____

_____

_____

_____

_____

■ What does it mean to you to confront a person "in a spirit of love"? Have you ever been confronted in this kind of way? Describe it. Have you ever confronted another person in this way? Explain.

_____

_____

_____

_____

Super You believes the myth: "I've always got to be super-happy." But are you always happy? Never depressed? Bubbling over with "Praise the Lord"? Is there never a time of struggle? Is there never a time when the heavens seem brass? When you do things out of sheer duty, without happy feelings?

In the Garden of Gethsemane, our Lord said to His disciples, "My soul is exceedingly troubled, even unto death." He was writhing on the ground; He was sweating profusely and undergoing a terrific struggle between His emotions and His will. His emotions were saying, "Father, You can do everything; take the cup away from Me if it's possible." But His will was as fixed as the magnet to the North Pole, and His will kept saying, "Not My will but Yours." And sometimes that same kind of struggle gives us an exceedingly troubled soul.

The word *happiness* has its roots in the word *happenings*. Happiness depends on happenings, on what happens to us, externals that we can't control. *Joy* is the right word for what we Christians are to expect. For *joy* is an internal word which has to do with relationships, not circumstances, not happenings. Joy is the inner calm at the eye of the storm; feelings can be stormy, but there can also be an inner sense of rightness to the will of God. But this does not mean that we have to go about with Super Self masks on, with smiling lips, sparkling teeth, and a "Praise the Lord!"

PERSONAL REFLECTION

■ Cite an example from your own life that demonstrates your understanding of the word *joy*.

_____

_____

_____

_____

As a Christian, you can be a realist. This means you don't need to be afraid to face the worst, the ugliest, the most painful. You don't have to be afraid to express your feelings of grief, sorrow, hurt, loneliness, struggle, even depression. Sometimes you may even experience depressive feelings like Elijah had after his greatest moment of triumph: "Oh, Lord, it is enough. Let me die."

There is a rugged honesty about the life of Jesus—every kind of emotion was so clearly recorded and freely expressed, without any sense of shame or guilt or imperfection. Take your pattern from Jesus, not from some mythical Super Self. You need never be afraid to express your real feelings and be your real self in Jesus Christ.

When you waste time and energy trying to be Super Self, you rob yourself of growth and the friendship of God. And you never let God accept and love the Real You for whom Christ died. This is the *only you* that God really knows and sees. Super You is an illusion of your imagination, a false image, an idol. I'm not sure that God even sees Super You. You can be yourself in Jesus, and you need not compare yourself to anyone else. He wants to heal *you* and to change *you* in order that Real You can grow up to be the person He intended you to be.

Super Self dies very hard, and the religious Super Self dies the hardest of all. If you find that you cling to it tenaciously, I hope you will hear the Holy Spirit saying, "Abandon it! Give it up! Then you and I can start the whole healing process of making the Real You."

PRAYERFUL REFLECTION

■ Have you robbed yourself of spiritual and emotional growth and the friendship of God because you've been trying to keep the Real You hidden from God and other people? Are you ready to let God *accept* and *love* the Real You for whom Christ died? Then tell Him so by journaling below a prayer to Him. Take off your Super Self masks (name the barriers that keep you hidden) and let God see and know the Real You—this is the *only you* God really knows and sees anyway.

_____

_____

_____

_____

_____

PERSONAL RENEWAL

■ In his book, *Nothing to Hide*, author William J. Rowley states, "Authenticity is the call of God. We are to 'walk in the light as He is in the light' (1 John 1:7). . . . Unfortunately, our experiences in life are often contrary to God's call. We learn early to project public images, to display ourselves as we wish others to see us, to hide who we really are" (Victor Books, p. 7). Jesus lived an authentic life. He clearly and freely expressed every kind of emotion without any sense of shame or guilt or imperfection. This week, read through the Gospel of Luke. As you are reading note every instance when Jesus clearly and freely expressed who He was to those He came in contact with. Jot down your observations in the Personal Journal sheet section at the end of this book. Let the life of Christ inspire you to be the Real You!

Why art thou cast down, O my soul? And why art thou disquieted in me? Hope thou in God: for I shall yet praise Him for the help of His countenance. O my God, my soul is cast down within me. . . . Deep calleth unto deep at the noise of Thy waterspouts: all Thy waves and Thy billows are gone over me. . . . My tears have been my meat day and night, while they continually say unto me, "Where is thy God?"

Psalm 42:5-7, 3

Chapter 10
Myths and Truths about Depression

Depression is a common experience among Christians. You may ask, "How can that be? A depressed Christian? The very words are contradictory; they are incompatible. If a person has been truly born of the Spirit, and certainly if he has been filled with the Spirit, then shouldn't it be impossible for him to be depressed? Surely, the fact that a Christian would be suffering from depression at all should be a sign that something is wrong, that something needs to be straightened out with the Lord. It must be a sign of sin in that person's life."

Now all of that may sound very good and very simple, but it does not stand the test of Scripture, the facts of Christian experience, or the truths about psychology. And it certainly does not square with the biographies of the saints.

Have you read some of David's psalms recently?

"Why art thou cast down, oh my soul?" (Ps. 42:5)

"O my God, my soul is cast down within me" (Ps. 42:6).

"Why art thou cast down? Hope in God; for I shall yet praise Him, who is the health of my countenance" (Ps. 43:5).

Or listened to Elijah? "O Lord, take away my life" (1 Kings 19:4).

Or Jonah? "It is better for me to die than to live" (Jonah 4:3).

Or heard Jesus' words in the Garden, as He was in pain and in prayer? "My soul is exceeding sorrowful, even unto death" (Matt. 26:38). Can you find better descriptions of depression—a depression in which the person almost despaired of life itself? Many of the depressive psalms speak of the countenance, the person's face, and how accurate those psalms are! The person who is depressed and dejected has a miserable countenance. He looks troubled, worried, unhappy, as if he is bearing the weight of the world on his shoulders.

PERSONAL
REFLECTION

■ Describe a time when you felt depressed. What brought about the depression? How did you deal with your depression? And how did other people around you respond to your depression?

_____

_____

_____

_____

■ Depression can be brought on by a number of different things, such as unhealthy eating patterns, lack of rest, stress, out-of-sorts relationships, anger turned inward, mood swings, personality, spiritual conflicts. Which of these things seem to most often lead to depression in your life? Is depression something you experience frequently, periodically, or rarely? Explain.

_____

_____

_____

_____

Another very common symptom of depression is tears. "My tears have been my meat day and night" (Ps. 42:3), says the psalmist. This is an amazingly accurate psychological statement! Depression often brings a loss of appetite. You just don't feel like eating. Because food seems repulsive, you begin to live on tears instead of food. "My tears have been my meat," and some of us could add, "Yes, and my vegetable, salad, dessert, and drink too." What's wrong? Unable to stop crying, you feed on despair, and that of course increases the depression.

The Scriptures are much more realistic and kind to us than some

Christians are, as they clearly show that it is possible for Christians to be very depressed. The biographies of the saints also deal with this. We often quote from John Wesley's great Aldersgate conversion experience, but I could show you several quotations that follow which almost seem to nullify it, as Wesley spoke out in depression, doubt, and dejection.

Samuel Logan Brengle, Portrait of a Prophet is the story of a great saint of the Salvation Army (Clarence W. Hall, The Salvation Army, Inc.). Brengle's classic works on holiness have been translated into scores of languages, and have been the means of leading millions of believers into a deeper life in Christ.

Speaking of Brengle, Hall wrote, "Then would come a battle with his feelings with the descent upon his mind of a constitutional melancholia" (p. 213). In a letter, Brengle wrote: "My nerves were ragged, frazzled, exhausted. And such gloom and depression fell upon me as I have never known, although depression is an old acquaintance of mine" (p. 214). In later life he suffered an injury to his head, when at a street meeting a drunk threw a brick at Brengle and hit him on the head. Complications from this injury increased the depression that had been a lifelong struggle, an "old acquaintance," as he called it. Yet was there ever a more sanctified saint than Samuel Logan Brengle?

Before a person can deal with depression, he must acknowledge it. And many a Christian, if he were completely honest about his emotions, would have to admit: "Yes, depression is an acquaintance of mine too. I know what you are talking about."

By denying their depression, many Christians add to their troubles. They add guilt on top of the depression and thereby double the problem. Let's say that a severe depression is equal to carrying one ton of emotional weight. That's about what it feels like, isn't it? To carry a ton on your back is bad, but you may have the strength for it. However, when you then add guilt by saying, "There's something wrong with me because I have this depression," you have then doubled the weight, and that's an impossible load for anyone to carry.

Depression is not necessarily a sign of spiritual failure. In the Scripture stories, some of the greatest depressions came as emotional letdowns following the greatest spiritual successes. This was true in the life of Elijah. After that greatest moment in his life, the triumph over the prophets of Baal on Mt. Carmel, what happened? The next time we see him he is sitting alone under the juniper tree, asking God to take his life. Abraham had a similar experience (Gen. 15). And many of us have too. Depression seems to be nature's emotional kickback. It is a reaction like the wallop from firing a gun of heavy caliber. It is nature's recoil, or perhaps the balance wheel in what C.S. Lewis calls "the law of undulation" in the human personality.

PERSONAL
REFLECTION

■ Can you think of a time when you experienced depression following the completion of a major project or event, a spiritual high point, or an extended time of personal decision-making? Describe it. What steps might you take in the future to prepare yourself for the emotional letdown of experiences like these?

_____

_____

_____

_____

_____

Unfortunately, some of our Christian friends can be our worst enemies at this point, offering us false and unrealistic advice. There are Christians who have little understanding about depression. Because their own personalities are not very subject to it, they fail to understand people who suffer depression. This can be especially cruel when two such people are married to one another. If a husband does not suffer much from depression but his wife does, he may have a difficult time appreciating her emotions and her moods. It can be a doubly cruel situation if he uses her depressed time to put a spiritual heavy on her. Or the wife on the husband, if the situation is reversed.

You can't assume that because you never suffer from depression, you are therefore more spiritual. C.S. Lewis once said that about half the times when we credit ourselves with virtue, it's really just a matter of temperament and constitution, and not of spirituality.

PERSONAL
REFLECTION

■ Are you a person whose personality is subject to depression? How have you learned to deal with this part of your personality? In what ways have you felt misunderstood because of it?

_____

_____

_____

_____

There is a depression that can come from the guilt of sin, from known disobedience and transgression. However, that kind is not what I am writing about. You may wonder, "How do I recognize the depression that comes from sin?" And that's a good question, especially if you are a perfectionist who suffers from an oversensitive conscience, from the tyranny of the oughts and the shoulds, or from a constant feeling of uneasiness, anxiety, and condemnation. Let me give you a general principle that I think can be very helpful. A concrete, specific feeling of guilt which can be related to a particular, precise act or attitude is generally a true and reliable feeling of guilt. And the emotions that follow can be real guilt and real depression for a real transgression.

PERSONAL REFLECTION

■ Do you identify with the statements Dr. Seamands makes about depression that comes from guilt? Try to think of an instance when you have experienced this kind of guilt. Jot it down. *NOTE: The purpose of this exercise is to help you get clear in your own thinking the difference between depression that comes from the guilt of sin and just plain depression.*

_____

_____

_____

_____

A vague, all-inclusive umbrella of systematic self-accusation, general overall feelings of anxiety and condemnation which cannot be pinpointed—these are generally signs of pseudo-guilt or just plain depression that has come from emotional sources. Sin may lead to depression, but all depression does not come from sin. The roots of depression often run deep and are very complicated, as complicated as many of the childhood hurts and scars that people carry into adulthood.

PERSONAL REFLECTION

■ As a point of contrast to the last writing exercise, think of a time when you experienced depression that stemmed from emotional sources. Briefly describe that experience below.

_____

_____

_____

_____

_____

_____

Depression is related to personality structure, physical makeup, body chemistry, glandular functions, emotional patterns, and learned feeling-concepts. As Christians we must realize and accept this. If all of us had the good common sense found in one of our most ancient nursery rhymes, we would be better off.

Jack Sprat could eat no fat,
His wife could eat no lean;
And so between them both,
They licked the platter clean.

Now this is an amazingly profound analysis of personality structure, believe it or not. Constitutionally, Jack Sprat and Mrs. Sprat are entirely different. Don't try to make them both eat the same way, or live the same way. That would be a violation of their personalities. They are both valuable human beings, and we presume that they love each other very much even though they are totally different in their makeup. I wish more preachers, teachers, evangelists, and especially parents would master the sound good sense of that nursery rhyme.

"Wait a minute," someone says. "You've forgotten that when we are in Christ, we are new creatures, and old things pass away. Don't regeneration and sanctification do away with old differences?" To this I must say, "No! Thank God, they do not!"

The new birth does not change your basic temperament. It can put within you, as Oswald Chambers loves to say, "the disposition of Jesus Christ," but it does not change your basic temperament. The fact that you have become a Christian does not mean that from now on you cease to live with yourself as yourself. Paul was still very much Paul after his conversion. Peter was still very much Peter, and John was John. They did not become other people. In God's plan, no two things are ever identical. No two snowflakes are alike. Through great variety within unity, God shows the wonder of His ways. We are each different, in temperament and personality structure. We see and feel, react to and interpret things individually.

PERSONAL REFLECTION

■ There are at least four temperament analysis tools available today to help us better understand our God-given personalities. The personality assessment exercise which follows is adapted from Gary Smalley and John Trent's "Today's Family Personality Overview" (Today's Family, *Love Is a Decision Seminar*, 1989, p. 37b). This assessment tool will help you more clearly understand your unique personality makeup and those of the significant others in your life.

Personality Overview

For each of the personality descriptions below, underline the words or phrases that describe a consistent character trait of yours. Total the number of words or phrases underlined for each personality type.

PERSONALITY "L" - "Let's do it now"
Takes charge, assertive, bold, enterprising, decision-maker, goal driven, enjoys challenges, determined, firm, purposeful, competitive, leader, self-reliant, adventurous.   TOTAL _____

PERSONALITY "O" - "Trust me, it will work out"
Takes risks, motivator, fun loving, very verbal, enjoys change, group-oriented, avoids detail, visionary, energetic, likes variety, promoter, creative, mixes easily, optimistic.   TOTAL _____

PERSONALITY "G" - "Let's keep things the way they are"
Loyal, even keel, enjoys routine, good listener, sympathetic, nurturing, tolerant, non-demanding, avoids conflict, dislikes change, adaptable, thoughtful, patient, deep relationship.
TOTAL _____

PERSONALITY "B" - "How was it done in the past?"
Deliberate, reserved, practical, factual, detailed, inquisitive, persistent, controlled, predictable, orderly, discerning, analytical, precise, scheduled.   TOTAL _____

Which personality type best described you? Did reading the descriptions help you better understand your unique self? Of the four personality types described above, PERSONALITY "L" and PERSONALITY "B" are more prone to depression.

The Apostle Paul reminded us: "We have this treasure in earthen vessels" (2 Cor. 4:7). By nature and temperament, some people are nervous, apprehensive, or easily frightened. They are oversensitive and their feelings are easily touched and changed. I sometimes wonder if Paul wasn't one of these. As strong as he was, he went to Corinth in "weakness and fear, with much trembling" (1 Cor. 2:3). He was a high-strung young man, "without were fightings, within were fears" (2 Cor. 7:5). Certainly this was true of young pastor Timothy. The entire Second Epistle to Timothy seems to have been written by Paul to pull Timothy out of depression. Brengle's biographer called him a "constitutional melancholic." People who are extremely introspective and sensitive often have the worst problems with depression.

Our failure to deal realistically with ourselves regarding depression is the root cause of much of our depression. If we have the idea that there is no connection between the *natural* (our temperament and personality structure) and the *supernatural* (our spiritual lives), we are seriously mistaken. Both our feelings and our faith operate through the same personality equipment. God does not come to us in special ways which bypass or short-circuit or side-track our personality equipment. He doesn't drill a hole in the tops of our skulls and with some magical, mystical funnel pour His grace into us. The mechanisms of our personalities which we use in faith are the same instruments through which our feelings operate.

Maybe we can understand it if we can think of one of these great big, expensive, combination centers with a TV in the middle, and a stereo record player, and radio. It's a beautiful piece of furniture. But if something goes wrong with some of the transistors in that vast assemblage, the audio system goes out. Why? All the components are all working through the same mechanism. If a connection burns out over here, or a condenser and some transistors go wrong over there, all three of the operations are going to be affected. Why? They are operating through the same system.

Depressions can come from sources outside the purely spiritual. They come because something has gone wrong with the equipment—perhaps in the physical, or in the balance of emotions and personality. Transistors have been affected, a connection has burned out, and it has affected even the spiritual life.

Let's return to Brengle, that very saintly man, as he writes about himself: "'Such gloom and depression fell upon me as I have never known. . . . God *seemed* nonexistent. The grave *seemed* my endless goal. Life lost all of its glory, charm, and meaning. . . . Prayer brought me no relief; indeed, I seemed to have lost the spirit of prayer and the power to pray'" (Hall, *Portrait of a Prophet*, p. 214).

PERSONAL
REFLECTION

■ Do you identify with the thoughts expressed by Brengle in the previous paragraph? Describe a time when you felt that way.

_____

_____

_____

_____

_____

To apply our previous illustration, there was nothing wrong with the sender; the love of God was still coming through. The radio station was sending out beautiful music, the TV transmitter was sending out the right images, but the only sound was static and the sight was TV "snow." Why? Because something had gone wrong with the receiving set.

That's what happened to Brengle. And notice how wise he was. In spite of his feelings, he realized God was still there. In every sentence he used the word *seemed*. "It *seemed* like God was nonexistent. . . . It *seemed* like the grave was my goal." And Brengle himself underlined the word *seemed*.

Have you ever experienced a complete change in your feelings? You go to bed one night and everything's fine. You wake up the next morning, and nothing's fine. Nothing you can think of accounts for it. Yesterday you were happy. You were looking forward to a great day. But something happened, and your responses are different. Your feelings, actions, interpretations of the very same things that took place yesterday are very different today. And you are not alone. God is there, but so is Screwtape. Satan is sitting there on the side of the bed, for he sees an opening to ride right into your personality. Why? Because Satan is of the spirit world, he already knows what you and I need to learn—that the same equipment which affects the natural also affects the spiritual. So Satan tries to turn temperamental depression into spiritual depression. Satan always wants to turn emotional depression into spiritual defeat. He wants to take a burned-out emotion in your receiving set and turn it into a burned-out trust. He's aware of your infirmities; and he knows the depths of your spirit and he comes riding that monorail right into the heart of your personality.

Do you know how Satan wants to win? He tries to get you to foul yourself out of the game. He wants to turn the natural mood of depression into spiritual defeat, doubt, and despondency.

PERSONAL
REFLECTION

■ In Ephesians 6:11, the Apostle Paul warns Christians to "Wear the full armor of God so that you can fight against the devil's evil tricks" (NCV). One of his tricks is to take a believer's natural mood of depression and turn it into spiritual defeat, doubt, and despondency. Describe a time when you found yourself feeling depressed and, consequently, spiritually defeated.

_____

_____

_____

_____

_____

_____

_____

_____

■ How can you combat Satan's attempts to defeat you spiritually through your natural depression? Look up Ephesians 6:13-18 and find out what God has already provided as a means of protection for you against Satan's assaults. Then write down two or three ideas you can use to combat Satan's spiritual accusations next time you feel depressed.

_____

_____

_____

_____

_____

_____

I urge you to accept your personality and acknowledge your temperament. Having truth in the inward parts means you no longer resist who you are. You stop fighting your temperament as an enemy and begin to accept it as a gift from God.

I personally spent many years fighting myself, trying to be someone else, battling my nervous, high-strung temperament, always feeling a bit angry about that, and trying to be someone else. The turning point came when I could accept myself as I am. For one day the Lord said, "Hey, this is all you've got! You're not going to get another personality. You'd better settle down and live with it and learn to do something with it.

"And, furthermore, if you'll just give the Real You into My hands—not Super You, which you are not—if you'll turn that over to Me, then you and I are going to get along fine, and I'll be able to use you as you are."

The first step in learning to live above depression is to accept yourself as you are. This does not mean you are to be controlled by your temperament. After conversion, the Holy Spirit is to be in control. But the Holy Spirit can only fill and control that which you acknowledge and surrender to Him. While you cannot change your temperament, you can allow it to be controlled by the Holy Spirit.

PERSONAL REFLECTION

■ What God-given part of your personality is most difficult for you to accept? Name any personality "flaws" you see in yourself. Afterward read Psalm 139. Then write a short prayer, expressing to God the confidence you feel in Him for designing you as He did.

_____

_____

_____

_____

_____

_____

We left Brengle in deep depression, and I don't want to leave him there—or you either. He said,

"Prayer brought no relief. Indeed, I seem to have lost the spirit of prayer and the power to pray. Then I remembered to give thanks and to praise God, though I felt no spirit of praise and thanksgiving. Feeling, except that of utter depression and gloom, was gone. But as I thanked God for the trial, it began to turn to blessing, light glimmered, grew very slowly, and then broke through the gloom. The depression passed away, and life was beautiful and desirable again, and full of gracious incomings once more" (Hall, _Portrait of a Prophet_, p. 214).

That's it! Brengle said, "I remembered." Paul wrote to Timothy, "I put you in remembrance." Tomorrow morning, remember that the love of God is not grounded in your feelings, nor in your performance, and not even in your love for Him. His love is grounded in His own faithfulness. "The steadfast love of the Lord never ceases, His mercies never come to an end; they are new every morning; great is Your faithfulness. 'The Lord is my portion,' says my soul, 'therefore will I hope in Him'" (Lam. 3:22-24, NRSV).

PRAYERFUL REFLECTION

■ Brengle discovered a key to overcoming depression—giving thanks and praising God. If we would only remember that the Lord's love never ceases, that His mercies never end, that each day is a new day, and that God is ever faithful, then we could move from depression to peace and joy. Next time you feel depressed, try this simple exercise: Make a list of things for which you are thankful, write them down, then recite your list of thanksgivings back to God, perhaps doing it in the form of a song. The Psalmist David did this often. (See Ps. 118.)

My Song of Praise

_____

_____

_____

_____

_____

_____

_____

_____

_____

_____

_____

_____

PERSONAL RENEWAL

■ The Book of Lamentations is a series of laments over the destruction of Jerusalem in 586 B.C. In the middle of the book, the theology of Lamentations reaches its apex as it focuses on the goodness of God. He is the Lord of hope (3:21, 24-25), of love (3:22), of faithfulness (3:23), of salvation (3:26). In spite of all evidence to the contrary, "His compassions never fail. They are new every morning; great is Your faithfulness" (3:22-23). Remind yourself of the goodness of God this week as you meditate on Lamentations 3:19-24 (NIV).

I remember my affliction and my wandering, the bitterness and the gall. I well remember them, and my soul is downcast within me. Yet this I call to mind and therefore I have hope: Because of the Lord's great love we are not consumed, for His compassions never fail. They are new every morning; great is Your faithfulness. I say to myself, "The Lord is my portion; therefore I will wait for Him."

This priceless treasure we hold, so to speak, in a common earthenware jar—to show that the splendid power of it belongs to God and not to us. We are handicapped on all sides, but we are never frustrated; we are puzzled, but never in despair. We are persecuted, but we never have to stand it alone: we may be knocked down but we are never knocked out!

This is the reason why we never collapse. The outward man does indeed suffer wear and tear, but every day the inward man receives fresh strength.

2 Corinthians 4:7-9, 16, PH

Chapter 11
Dealing with Depression

By honestly acknowledging your feelings about depression, you are not adding to God's information about you. He knows those feelings. Through His Son He experienced them as He walked in your moccasins, and He is with you to understand and to help. As you admit and examine your depression, you can go on to take positive steps toward healing.

You have physical, emotional, and spiritual limitations, and you need to stay within them. Have you been getting enough sleep? Occasionally, we all are called on to go without sufficient rest; we have reserves on which we can draw. But to make the exception the rule means you will live regularly with fatigue. If you do so, I can guarantee that you will suffer from chronic, and perhaps even clinical and pathological depression. You will feel like the man who said he not only had an identity crisis, but also an energy crisis. He didn't know who he was and he was just too tired to find out!

Let me answer one question before you ask it—no, it makes no difference if you are in the Lord's service! God does not suspend His laws and make cosmic pets of preachers, missionaries, high achievers, and overcommitted church workers. They still come under the laws He has built into our bodies and emotions. And you cannot regularly violate those laws and expect to get by with it. What kind of load are you carrying? Who do you think you are, anyhow? God? That is one of the perfectionist's problems, you know.

Are you eating properly and regularly? My niece, who is a doctor, at one time specialized in emergency-room treatment. I asked her, "What do you do when depressed people who have attempted suicide are brought into the emergency room?"

She surprised me when she said, "Well, sometimes the first thing we do is to feed them, often a steak dinner. They are generally low in protein. We often discover that they have not eaten properly for two or three days. Their protein level is very low; therefore, their energy level is low, and their depression level is high." There are Christians who consistently neglect the physical area of their lives and then wonder why they are depressed.

Did you ever think that perhaps your depression is God's built-in cruise control for your life? Trying to slow you down, trying to balance out your emotions, because you regularly try to live above realistic possibilities? When the slave-driver of perfectionism propels you with that sense of "ought," you overstrain your emotional motor, and pay the price for it in chronic depression.

PERSONAL REFLECTION

■ Are YOU living beyond your physical means? Do a quick, personal inventory, noting any areas where you may be living beyond your physical means at present.

My Physical Limits
How much sleep do you normally require to feel rested? Have you been getting the sleep your body requires? If not, why not?

_____

_____

_____

_____

Are you eating properly and regularly? Monitor your eating patterns for a day, taking time to jot down *when* and *what* you eat throughout the day. Are these your normal eating patterns? If not, why not?

_____

_____

_____

_____

When was the last time you had a thorough physical examination? How about a dental checkup? (Note the date of each exam below.)

What, if anything, keeps you from maintaining these aspects of your physical well-being?

_____

_____

_____

_____

Are you getting regular physical exercise? Describe your weekly exercise routine. What would you like to do differently in this area of your life? Write down two measureable, achieveable exercise goals for yourself.

_____

_____

_____

_____

_____

The things that happen to you are not as important as the ways you respond to those events. And there are certain responses that can produce a chain reaction leading to emotional and spiritual depression.

Has something happened which has been a blow to your ego? Has someone disappointed you badly? When you tried so hard, did you get a B+ instead of an A? You may have had a deep experience or hurt or loss, a home broken by death or divorce. Or, on a lesser level, but just as hurtful at a youthful stage in life, is a breakup with a boyfriend or a girlfriend. I've had many a depressed young person come to me and say, "My friends are all jumping on me, saying, 'You shouldn't feel this way if you are a real Christian.'" How cruel we can be to our young people with such unrealistic standards! Leaving familiar, safe, comfortable places, roots, and faces, coming into strangeness and newness—these are blows which can lead to depression.

Sometimes it is an unusual blow to our selfhood that catches us off guard! We won the major battle; we took on the tanks, the heavy artillery, but then we got picked off by some little sniper in the bushes. That's the way it was with the Prophet Elijah. He confronted 400 priests in one of the most dramatic showdown battles in all of history. And then, a caustic, snippy remark by Jezebel, Ahab's wife, got to him: "You go tell that prophet that I'll make his life so miserable that by sunset he will wish he were dead!" (See 1 Kings 19:2.)

That's where it all began: "If you're not out of town by sunset. . . ." Elijah was feeling so good that the sniper's bullet caught him off guard. He was drained from hours of prayer, struggle, and fatigue. When Jezebel's sniping hit him, he went into suicidal depression. Then God used the emergency room technique on him. First, He sent the ravens to feed Elijah some protein; this was followed by some much needed sleep. Then God reoriented Elijah's perception: "You're not the only one, My friend; there are 7,500 who are with you. You forgot that." Before long, Elijah's emotions and spirit had been restored to normal.

PERSONAL REFLECTION

■ Are YOU living beyond your emotional and spiritual means? Do a quick, personal inventory, noting any areas where you may be living beyond your emotional or spiritual means at present.

My Emotional & Spiritual Limits

Has something happened recently which has been a blow to your ego? Has someone badly disappointed you? Have you experienced some kind of personal failure? Are you grieving over a broken or lost relationship? Describe anything that may be draining you of emotional energy at present.

_____

_____

_____

_____

_____

Overcommitment is the result of not being able to say no to others. Have you become overwhelmed with outside commitments at work, church, in the community, helping friends and or family?

How might these overcommitments be sabotaging your emotional and spiritual well-being at this time in your life?

_____

_____

_____

_____

_____

I see three primary reactions that lead to depression. They are *indecision, anger,* and a sense of unfairness or *injustice.*

1. Indecision. When a decision is needed, do you consistently put off making it? Is this your standard way of coping? If it is, you have a built-in depressor that will destroy your peace of mind and increase your feeling of being trapped. Many depressed people feel a sense of powerlessness: "I'm trapped. I don't see any way out." You could be using the same energy, not to postpone the decision, but to make it and carry it out. Using your energy to make a constructive decision is a good way to avoid depression.

Do you postpone decisions because you are afraid to say no? Because you are afraid to hurt someone? There are some situations you can never get out of without hurting someone. When you postpone dealing with them, you end up hurting people twice as much, and become depressed yourself. Are you afraid to say yes? Afraid of responsibility or of risk? If you sit and look at the two roads and go back and forth, you literally end up being double-minded. And the double-minded person, said James, is unstable in all his ways. (See James 1:8.) Indecision is often the precursor of depression.

PERSONAL
REFLECTION

■ Have you been putting off making a decision about something in your life? What is the decision regarding? Why do you think you are postponing making this particular decision?

_____

_____

_____

_____

_____

_____

2. *Anger.* The most concise definition of depression I know is this: "Depression is frozen rage." If you have a consistently serious problem with depression, you have not resolved some area of anger in your life. As surely as the night follows the day, depression follows unresolved, repressed, or improperly expressed anger.

PERSONAL
REFLECTION

■ Getting in touch with unresolved, repressed, or improperly expressed anger can be a frightening experience for the "good Christian perfectionist" who has been taught that anger is bad. What do you most fear about getting in touch with the hidden anger in your life?

_____

_____

_____

_____

3. *Injustice.* Perfectionists have a very disproportionate sense of justice and injustice. They feel a deep need to right the wrongs of the world, to correct things, to pull up the weeds that are growing with the wheat. Now, that feeling is valuable; it exists in every reformer, in every preacher and missionary; and to some degree it should be in every Christian. That sense of injustice surrendered, cleansed, and controlled by the Holy Spirit can be a useful instrument in the hands of God "for spreading scriptural holiness and reforming the nation," as John Wesley said. But out of hand, out of balance, with the basic anger problem behind it unresolved, the sense of injustice is very destructive, producing depression and disrupting good personal relationships.

I have rarely met a depressive perfectionist who didn't have a terrific sense of injustice and unfairness. The only answer to this deep anger against the injustices of life is forgiveness. Who most often needs to be forgiven? Parents and family members. So often, the roots of depression are buried in the subsoil of early family life. And unless you learn to deal honestly with those angry roots, to face your resentment and forgive, you'll be living in a greenhouse where depression is sure to flourish.

■ What deep injustices of life are keeping you emotionally buried in the past? These roots of bitterness most often lead to depression and keep you stuck in a dark and lonely place. If you will courageously identify those hurts and bring them to the light of God's forgiveness, then you can find peace and freedom from the past. Do your best right now to identify any painful hurts of your life. As you recall them, write them down on the roots in the illustration below.

IDENTIFIABLE ROOTS OF BITTERNESS IN MY LIFE

Two sisters, Mary and Martha, were opposites. Mary was an outgoing and vivacious blonde. Martha was a quiet and very talented brunette. Martha came to talk because a dating relationship, the best in her life so far, was developing. It was also bringing out a whole parcel of emotional problems, a lot of depression, and an angry, faultfindingness toward the young man. She wanted to love him and was learning to, but was shocked to realize she also wanted to pick him to pieces and hurt him. As she looked back, she realized that this was her dating pattern from years past, and it scared her.

As we talked, a lot of deep resentments came to the surface and she began to deal with them. Some were feelings toward Mother and Dad, and those were forgiven so that love could replace the anger.

But one day it became very obvious that Martha's real problem was Mary. And all of a sudden the angry memories marched across the screen of her imagination. As far back as she could remember, life was comparisons—comparisons by parents, teachers, friends, preachers, and neighbors.

As we began praying for the healing of those memories, and as she told God she was willing to forgive and to be forgiven and to let God change her feelings, it was as if the Holy Spirit pulled back a curtain, revealing to Martha a whole chain of insights. And in her praying she began to cry out, "O Lord! I realize that everything I have ever said or thought or done or aimed at has been in reference to Mary. She has ruled my life; she has been my obsession; she's almost taken over Your place in my life!"

Martha had never chosen a dress or a course in college or a boyfriend or set a goal, or made any choice without feeling that she was in competition with Mary. And all the hidden hurts and anger had emotionally enslaved her to her older sister. What a struggle it was to let go, to forgive what she felt were the injustices of the comparisons, and the favoritisms which may or may not have been shown. Martha had a prayer battle that went on for well over an hour. At the end, she was exhausted; and so was I. But after that time of struggling prayer, Martha was able to truly forgive; she was released and set free from the hateful, competitive, angry little girl inside of her who had never grown because she had been frozen.

The best part of the story came months later when she said, "You know, I've literally been born all over again. My depressions are normal mood changes now; none of those black pits I used to have. And best of all, I've discovered myself to be a totally different person than I thought I was. I'm free! I've got my own ideas, my own tastes. I make my own choices now, and set my own goals. I'm just so happy being me!"

Even her facial expression had changed, and in time Martha became a whole person, free to love. Why? Because she had faced her anger and her sense of unfairness, and had let God's love wash them all out.

PERSONAL
REFLECTION

■ What's YOUR story? If you were to tell it right now would it look anything like Martha's? Note below any ways in which your story resembles Martha's.

_____

_____

_____

_____

_____

Is there frozen anger somewhere in your life? Toward parents? Family members? Are you angry at God? So many people need to forgive God, not because He has ever done anything wrong, but because they have held Him responsible. It is time to face up to your true feelings and resolve them in an understanding of His love.

You may need to forgive your marriage partner for past mistakes. But to forgive is also a present extension of grace to the person himself. Forgive your partner for just being the way he is or she is—unable to meet some of your needs. Some of the most serious marital depressions arise when a husband or a wife thinks, *But, God, I have a right to feel this way! I ought to feel this way because she/he. . . .* And when we say we have a *right* to feel cheated and resentful and betrayed, we are on the road to depression!

You may be depressed because you hold on to anger and refuse to forgive people who have authority over you. Granted, they may have misused their authority. They may have done wrong. But you need to forgive those whom God in His providence has allowed to have authority over you. If you refuse, don't be surprised if you and depression become close companions.

When Paul wrote to the church at Rome, he said, "Never take vengeance into your own hands, my dear friends: stand back and let God punish if He will. For it is written: 'Vengeance belongeth unto Me: I will recompense. . . . If thine enemy hunger, feed him; if he thirst, give him to drink.' . . . Don't allow yourselves to be overpowered with evil. Take the offensive—overpower evil with good!" (Rom. 12:19-21, PH) The correcting of the injustices and the unfairnesses and the hurts of this world is God's business, and He warns, "Keep out of MY business!"

However, He does invite you to join Him in His work of forgiving and loving. "Be kind, tenderhearted one to another, forgiving one another," as God would say it—"even as *I* for Christ's sake have forgiven you" (Eph. 4:32). Get out of the setting right and getting even business, and into the forgiving and the loving business.

When you surrender your anger and oversensitivity to injustice and unfairness, you won't have trouble with self-pity, and your depressions will lessen immediately.

PERSONAL REFLECTION

■ Facing our anger and resentments honestly and choosing to forgive those who have hurt us, relieves us of the need to set things straight or get even. Complete the following inventory, putting a check mark next to each person you may be harboring resentment toward. Then in the lined space provided, make a list of incidents you can recall that have created resentment in you. *NOTE: If you need more space to write, use the Personal Journal sheets that have been provided in the back of this book.*

Resentments Inventory

□ Mother □ Grandparent □ Boyfriend □ Spiritual Authority
□ Father □ Spouse □ Girlfriend □ Authority Figure
□ Sister □ Child □ Employer □ God
□ Brother □ Friend □ Employee □ Other

I feel resentful toward _____

What caused this resentment is _____

_____

_____

This resentment has effected my life by _____

_____

_____

I feel resentful toward _____

*What caused this resentment is*_____

_____

_____

*This resentment has effected my life by*_____

_____

_____

It may surprise you to know that Martin Luther wrote a great deal about depression. Because of his unhappy childhood, because of an overbearing strict, religious upbringing, Martin Luther had a constant battle with low self-esteem and depression. He offered a lot of wonderfully up-to-date suggestions about meeting this problem. Let me share a few of his, and some of my own, which I have found to be most helpful.

1. Avoid being alone. When you are depressed you don't want to be around people. You want to withdraw. But withdrawing means isolation, and isolation during depression means alienation. Force yourself to be with people. This is one of the major areas where you have a definite choice in your depression.

2. *Seek help from others*. During depression your perceptions change. A little hill becomes a great mountain. But real friends can help you see its true height in perspective. You can no more pull yourself out of depression than you can get yourself out of quicksand by pulling at your own hair. Seek out people and situations which generate joy. Here again your choice is definitive.

3. *Sing! Make music*. This was the only cure for King Saul's moods of depression. The harmony and beauty of David's music lifted King Saul's spirit of depression (1 Sam. 16:14-23).

4. *Praise and give thanks*. All the saints of the centuries agree on this one. It was Brengle's way out. When he couldn't feel God's presence or really pray, he would thank God for the leaf on the tree or the beautiful wing of a bird. For simple, everyday things. In essence Paul told Timothy: "Remember, and be thankful" (2 Tim. 1). To the Thessalonians he didn't say, "*Feel* thankful for everything," but "*In* everything *give* thanks" (1 Thes. 5:18).

5. *Lean heavily on the power of God's Word*. God can use any portion of the Scriptures to minister to you during times of depression, but throughout the centuries His people have found the psalms to be the most beneficial. This is because the psalmist is the one most familiar with and open to the whole range of depressive emotions. Out of the 150 Psalms, there are 48 which can speak to your condition. Here is a list I often give out: 6, 13, 18, 23, 25, 27, 31, 32, 34, 37, 38, 39, 40, 42, 43, 46, 51, 55, 57, 62, 63, 69, 71, 73, 77, 84, 86, 90, 91, 94, 95, 103, 104, 107, 110, 116, 118, 121, 123, 124, 130, 138, 139, 141, 142, 143, 146, 147.

The most profitable procedure is to read them out loud. This allows the psalmist to become your contemporary, expressing both his and your feelings of abandonment, despair, melancholy, and his (and I trust, your) affirmation of faith and hope in God.

6. *Rest confidently in the presence of God's Spirit*. The psalmist repeatedly affirmed the secret of deliverance from depression. He encouraged himself, "Hope thou in God; for I shall yet praise Him for the *help of His countenance*" (Ps. 42:5, italics mine). It is the assurance of God's "countenance"—His face, that is the guarantee of His personal presence.

Jesus used this same basic concept when comforting His deeply depressed disciples on the eve of His departure. "I shall ask the Father to give you Someone else to stand by you, to be with you always. . . . I am not going to leave you alone in the world—I am coming to you. In a very little while . . . you will see Me, because I am really alive" (John 14:16, 18-19, PH).

I read the experience of a man who underwent open heart surgery. He said:

The day before the surgery an attractive nurse came into my room to visit. She took hold of my hand, and told me to feel it and hold it. I thought that was a great idea! "Now," she said, "during the surgery tomorrow you will be disconnected from your heart and you will be kept alive only by virtue of certain machines. And when your heart is finally restored and the operation is over and you are reconnected, you will eventually awaken in a special recovery room. But you will be immobile for as long as six hours. You may be unable to move, or speak, or to even open your eyes, but you will be perfectly conscious and you will hear and you will know everything that is going on around you. During those six hours I will be at your side and I will hold your hand exactly as I am doing now. I will stay with you until you are fully recovered.   Although you may feel absolutely helpless, when you feel my hand, you will know that I will not leave you."

It happened exactly as the nurse told me. I awoke, and could do nothing. But I could feel the nurse's hand in my hand for hours. And that made the difference.

Jesus' favorite word for His promised presence in the Holy Spirit is *Paraclete*—"the One called alongside." Engrave the words of Jesus on your mind until they will be such a part of you that during the lowest depression you will know, regardless of how you feel, that He is with you.

Jesus knew that [His disciples] wanted to ask Him what He meant, so He said to them: "Are you trying to find out from each other what I meant when I said, 'In a little while you will not see Me, and again, in a little while you will see Me'? I tell you truly that you are going to be both sad and sorry while the world is glad. Yes, you will be deeply distressed, but your pain will turn into joy. . . . Now you are going through pain, but I shall see you again and your hearts will thrill with joy—the joy that no one can take away from you—and on that day you will not ask Me any questions" (John 16:19-20, 22-23, PH).

PRAYERFUL REFLECTION

■ The pathway to emotional healing in our lives oftentimes takes us through dark valleys. In 1676, a tinker named John Bunyan wrote a classic tale about a pilgrim, named Christian, who takes a journey from the City of Destruction to the Celestial City. Christian experiences many difficulties along the way, perhaps the most challenging being what he faces as he makes his way through the Valley of the Shadow of Death. The author describes it this way: "I saw in my dream that Christian had now to enter another Valley—the darkest he had yet encountered. It was a very lonely place, where there was no water. No one lived there, and its silence was the silence of the grave. Here Christian was to be more sternly tested than ever before" (*Dangerous Journey*, Marshall Morgan & Scott, p. 59). Does your depression feel like a dark valley to you?

Then remember what the psalmist said, "Even though I walk through the valley of the shadow of death, I will fear no evil, for You are with me." The *Paraclete*—"the One called alongside" is ALWAYS with you. Take a few minutes right now to thank Him for His abiding presence in your life.

_____

_____

_____

_____

_____

_____

PERSONAL RENEWAL

■ Renew your thoughts and feelings by meditating on Psalm 23 this week. Be assured of the Holy Spirit's abiding presence and comfort in your life as you read this psalm.

The Lord is my shepherd, I shall not be in want. He makes me lie down in green pastures, He leads me beside quiet waters, He restores my soul. He guides me in paths of righteousness for His name's sake. Even though I walk through the valley of the shadow of death, I will fear no evil, for You are with me; Your rod and Your staff, they comfort me. You prepare a table before me in the presence of my enemies. You anoint my head with oil; my cup overflows. Surely goodness and love will follow me all the days of my life, and I will dwell in the house of the Lord forever.

For we know that the whole creation groans and suffers the pains of childbirth together until now. And not only this, but also we ourselves, having the firstfruits of the Spirit, even we ourselves groan within ourselves, waiting eagerly for our adoption as sons, the redemption of our body. . . .

And in the same way the Spirit also helps our weakness; for we do not know how to pray as we should, but the Spirit Himself intercedes for us with groanings too deep for words; and He who searches the hearts knows what the mind of the Spirit is, because He intercedes for the saints according to the will of God. And we know that God causes all things to work together for good to those who love God, to those who are called according to His purpose.

Romans 8:22-23, 26-28, NASB

Chapter 12
Healed Helpers

We come now to an important part of the healing process, perhaps the most important of all, because it reveals God's healing power at its greatest triumph—His ability to take human hurts and turn them to our good and His glory.

■ As you begin this final chapter in *Healing for Damaged Emotions*, take just a minute to reflect back over the past twelve weeks. Do you have a clear sense that God's purposes are being fulfilled in your life as you struggle through the issues related to your own healing process? Write a short thank-you to God for the work of healing He has begun, and will complete, in your life.

We have dealt with various kinds of grace. Let us now look at what I like to call *recycling grace*. I once visited a city where they had a great recycling plant for garbage. In this recycling plant the garbage was turned into useful fuel for energy. In a similar way

God's recycling grace takes our infirmities, our damaged emotions, and the garbage of our lives and turns them from curses that cripple into means for growth and instruments to be used in His service.

There is no place in Scripture that deals with this more profoundly or beautifully than Romans 8:18-28. While this passage certainly has a wider application, I want to apply it particularly to the way God can change people who are hurting into healed helpers.

Paul began by recognizing the fact that we live in a fallen, imperfect, and suffering world. Immediately, someone may object: "I get tired of you preachers always falling back on this. Why does there have to be so much pain and suffering in this world?"

The important words in the protest are *this world*, and they are precisely Paul's point. We suffer because it is *this world*, not some dream world that we would like to have, some utopia that we may fantasize about and wish to live in. We live in *this world*—after the Fall, this side of Eden, this paradise-lost world where sin entered by the choices of God's children. In *this world* where evil spoiled God's original perfect blueprint: marred it, scarred it, defaced and disfigured it. In *this world*, where now, instead of God's perfect and intentional will, we often—perhaps always—have to settle for His permissive and conditional will. Paul was really saying, "Face reality! You cannot push history back before the Fall; you cannot live in a dream world." He then said that *all* of this world, the total creation from the inanimate to the human, is defective. The world is suffering, hoping for a new birth, a final redemption for nature and humanity, in which we will be new persons with new bodies and minds, and everything set right.

Paul was not saying that God *needs* our sins and our infirmities, our failures and our blunders, to work out His designs and His will in this world. But in this fallen world, these are just about the only materials through which He can work out His providential and permissive will. If we were able to trace all human damages and hurts, we would find that ultimately they are the result of someone's sin, perhaps even generations back. If we could trace a hurt far enough, we would see that what comes through as infirmities and damaged emotions was passed along through imperfect genes and imperfect parenting and imperfect performance.

So often when someone in my office has been pouring out a fearful story of hurts, he will stop and say, "But one of the things that helped is that later I got to know his or her parents or grandparents, the family. I found out what had happened to him and how damaged and destroyed he was. Then I began to understand and even to feel compassion." I am always glad to hear that, for I know that compassion can bring acceptance, and acceptance can give birth to love.

PERSONAL REFLECTION

■ What aspects of your own life evidence that God's original perfect blueprint for your life has been marred, scarred, defaced, or disfigured in some way? Describe specific "marrings" in your life as you see them.

_____

_____

_____

_____

_____

■ The hidden, hurtful parts of our past that we fail to acknowledge, are destined to be repeated. What, if any, family "secrets" (shameful acts of the past that are never talked about in the present) are you aware of in your own family of origin? In your life today as an adult?

_____

_____

_____

_____

_____

■ In what ways have the hurts of your past cultivated in your heart more compassion for others who have also suffered?

_____

_____

_____

_____

_____

_____

Paul applied the profound theology of Romans 8:18-28 to a very practical area—the place where we live with our damaged emotions and hangups. "The Holy Spirit helps us in our infirmities," in our weaknesses (Rom. 8:26). Thank God! He doesn't leave us alone; we are not abandoned to our paltry resources to somehow struggle through all this mess, to live defeated lives. No! For our Wounded Healer, our High Priest, Jesus Christ, is "touched with the feelings of our infirmities." Jesus, the Son of God, identified with us humans when He became the Son of Man. He not only knows our infirmities, but also our feelings. He understands the pain of rejection, the anxiety of separation, the terror of loneliness and abandonment, the dark clouds of depression. These infirmities, these cripplings and weaknesses, He knows, He understands, He feels. He is our Wounded Healer, the One "wounded for our transgressions," who "bore our iniquities and our infirmities."

Because Christ is the Wounded Healer, because He does fully understand, when He got ready to leave this world, He promised that He would not leave His friends alone, but would come to them by sending the Comforter, the Paraclete. (See John 14:16-18.) *Para* means "alongside," and *kaleo* means "to call." "I will send you One whom you can call upon who will come alongside and *help* you with your infirmities."

PERSONAL REFLECTION

■ Can you think of anyone in your life at present who, when called upon, is able to empathize with your feelings of rejection, separation, loneliness, abandonment, and depression because he or she has been through similar experiences? Who is it? Describe a time when that person came alongside and helped you through an emotionally troubled time in your life.

_____

_____

_____

_____

_____

_____

■ Now describe your experience with the Holy Spirit as the Paraclete, the Comforter. How has He come alongside and helped you during emotionally troubled times? How easy is it for you to depend on Him for the comfort He promises to provide during those times? Why?

_____

_____

_____

_____

_____

We must take a look at the Greek word for *help*. It's a combination of three words: *sun*—"along with, together"; *anti*—"on the opposite side"; and *lambano*—"to take hold of." When you put them together, *sunantilambanotai* means "to take hold of together with us over on the other side." Did you ever get excited over a Greek word? You should when you think of this one! "I will send you a Paraclete who comes alongside when you call, who will take hold of, together with you, on the other side."

It helps to get even more technical in our word analysis, for this word is in the indicative mood and represents a fact. It is in the middle voice, indicating that the Holy Spirit is doing the action; it is in the present tense, that speaks of habitual, continuous action. He is always there!

Here is one of the great works of the comforting, counseling Paraclete—He is always available to take hold on the other side of our crippling infirmity, our damaged emotion, our painful hangup. He doesn't leave us because we are damaged or imperfect in our performance. He is exactly the opposite from the misconceived caricature of the God which the perfectionist imagines—the God who is always whispering, "Come on now! Try a little harder! You can do better than that! Measure up and I will love you!" The Paraclete is the God who understands, who sees we are carrying a burden too heavy for us, who realizes we cannot make it on our own, who comes alongside and takes hold of the heavy burden and its pain and helps us to lift it, enabling us to carry our crippling infirmity. What a beautiful picture!

PERSONAL REFLECTION

■ Is there any crippling weakness, damaged emotion, or painful hangup you are carrying on your own at this time? Describe what it is. Then imagine the Holy Spirit coming alongside you to take hold of your heavy burden and pain and help you carry it. How do you feel knowing the Holy Spirit is always there, continuously helping you bear your emotional burden?

_____

_____

_____

_____

_____

_____

The verb *sunantilambanotai* is found in only one other place in the New Testament, in Luke 10:40. Mary was sitting at the feet of Jesus, enjoying His love and His teachings. Martha was scurrying about in the kitchen, doing all the work by herself. She was also doing a slow burn, getting madder by the minute. Finally, she burst through the door onto the front porch where Jesus and Mary were sitting and blurted out, "Jesus, will You please speak to Mary and tell her to come in here and *sunantilambano* me? Tell her to come in here and do her share and get hold of the other side. I can't do it all myself." That's the picture in this word: the Holy Spirit helping us, taking hold of the other side.

Here is the good news of the Gospel for people with damaged emotions:

■ God loves us, not because we are good, but because we need His love in order to be good.

■ Christ, our High Priest, bore our sins and our infirmities, not because we are good, but because we need His love and acceptance in order to be good.

■ The Holy Spirit offers us His continuous enabling presence and power, not because we are good, but because we need Him in order to be good. What good news!

Here is the complete provision of the grace of God. The *Father's* unconditional and accepting love, the *Son's* complete identification as our High Priest and Wounded Healer with our sins and our infirmities, and the *Spirit's* daily loving, lifting help.

And how does the Holy Spirit help us with these crippling infirmities? "For we do not know how to pray as we should, but the Spirit Himself intercedes for us" (Rom. 8:26, NASB). Only the Holy Spirit truly knows the mind of God. And only the Holy Spirit truly understands us. Because He understands the inside of us and understands the inside of the heart of God, He knows how to get these two together. And so the Spirit Himself intercedes for us with groanings too deep to be uttered. He intercedes for us in agreement with the will of God.

THE HEALING WORK OF THE HOLY SPIRIT

"He who searches the hearts knows what the mind of the Spirit is" (v. 27, NASB). If you will take the word *hearts* and roughly translate it "subconscious minds," I think you will understand what Paul was saying. In this deep inner self—this great storehouse of our memories where our hurts and pains lie buried too deep for ordinary prayer, sometimes too deep for any audible prayer—this is where emotional healing takes place by the work of the Holy Spirit. This is where the soothing Balm of Gilead cleans out old wounds, brings forgiveness, repairs damages, and pours in the love of God to bring healing. The Paraclete not only comes alongside, but He also comes inside.

PERSONAL
REFLECTION

■ Describe a time when the Spirit searched your *heart* (subconscious mind) and brought to the light a deep hurt or pain in you that needed to be healed. What was the result of Him revealing that truth to you about your own brokenness?

_____

_____

_____

_____

_____

The best is yet to be! Too often we quote Romans 8:28, out of context. It is the final step in this whole corrective sequence: "And we know that God causes all things to work together for good to those who love God" (NASB). The older version of this verse can be misleading: "All things work together for good. . . ." Unfortunately the *things* do not; they may even work against us. But *God* works in and through the things, causing circumstances to work out for our good. That's different, for it turns the emphasis from fate to a Father! From things and happenstance to God, a Person of love and design. That God causes all things to work together for good is the greatest part of the entire healing process; that He can change hurtful insights to helpful outreach is the greatest miracle of all.

Without this, the healing could not be considered total, for total healing is more than soothing painful memories, more than forgiving and being forgiven of harmful resentments, even more than the reprogramming of our minds. Healing is the miracle of God's recycling grace, where He takes it all and makes good come out of it, where He actually recycles our hangups into wholeness and usefulness.

PERSONAL
REFLECTION

■ Dr. Seamands aptly reminds us that the greatest miracle in the healing of damaged emotions is that God "can change hurtful insights to helpful outreach." How have you evidenced this in your own life? Recount specific instances when you saw God use your healing process to help others find healing in their lives.

_____

_____

_____

_____

_____

_____

_____

This doesn't mean that all of the harmful things we've been describing were God's intentional will for our lives. God is not the *Author* of all events, but He is the *Master* of all events. This means that nothing has ever happened to you that God cannot and will not use for good if you will surrender it into His hands and allow Him to work.

God does not change the actual, factual nature of the evil which occurs. Humanly speaking, nothing can change this; it is still evil, tragic, senseless, and perhaps unjust and absurd. But God can change the *meaning* of it for your total life. God can weave it into the design and purpose of your life, so that it all lies within the circle of His redeeming and recycling activity.

God is the great Alchemist who, if you will let Him, will turn it all into spiritual gold. He is the Master Weaver who can take every damage, every hurt, every crippling infirmity and weave them all into His design—yes, even though their threads were spun by evil, ignorant, and foolish hands!

When you cooperate with the Holy Spirit in this process of deep prayer and inner healing, then God will not only remake and recondition you, He will not only reweave the design, but will also recycle it into a means of serving others. Then you will be able to look at it and say, "It is the Lord's doing and marvelous in our eyes."

PERSONAL REFLECTION

■ What new and beautiful design do you think the Master Weaver is making of *your* life? Try to picture how God might be using the emotional damage, hurts, and crippling weaknesses of your life to create a beautiful new design. Using colored pencils, crayons, or colored markers, draw a piece of fabric that expresses what you believe God is reweaving as the result of His healing work in your life.

_____

_____

I AM THE MASTER WEAVERS WORK OF ART

Betty and her husband came to counsel with me. I knew that they were a deeply committed Christian couple preparing for Christian service, and that they had a solid marriage. However, recently there had been some relational difficulties between them and an increasing sense of depression on Betty's part. Her tears flowed freely that first time we met together—tears which surprised her. She thought she had turned them off many years ago, but now they seemed to turn themselves on, uncontrollably and embarrassingly.

When Betty came back the next time, she began to share her story with me. Her parents had been forced to get married because her mother was pregnant with her. It was an undesired marriage and Betty had been unwanted. (May I just say parenthetically that if this is true of your life, then sometime you need to come to peaceful terms with it.)

When Betty was three and a half, her mother became pregnant again. However, her father had impregnated another woman at about the same time. This led to serious conflict and finally to divorce. Betty's memory of all this was incredibly clear. She vividly remembered that final day when her father walked out the door and left home. She remembered being in her own little crib-bed in the room when it happened; hearing the vicious quarrel and the terrifying moment when he left. It had left an aching, malignant core of pain deep within her. It was while we were in the midst of reexperiencing that incident during a time of prayer for the healing of her memories, that the Lord took us right back into that crib.

Jesus can do that, you know, because all time is present with Him. He is the One who said, "Before Abraham was, I am" (John 8:58). Our memories are all there before Him who is the Lord of time. During the healing time, Betty uttered a wracking, wrenching cry of pain which had been buried for many years. I said to her, "Betty, if you could have said something to your father from your crib, at that moment—what would you have said?" And suddenly the Holy Spirit brought back up into her memory exactly what she had felt in that moment of total desolation. And she cried out, not in the voice of a young adult, but the sobs of a three-and-a-half-year-old, "Oh, Daddy, please don't leave me!" And all the terror and the pain of that moment came out "with sounds too deep to be uttered."

Later, as we prayed together, it dawned on me that if we were to translate Christ's cry of dereliction from the cross ("My God, My God, why hast Thou forsaken Me?") into a paraphrase for a child, we couldn't improve on Betty's words: "Daddy, please don't leave me!" And suddenly, I realized that because of what Jesus experienced on that cross, He understands the cries heard so often in our day, the cries of millions of little children, "Daddy," or "Mommy, please don't leave me!" But they *do* leave. And the Wounded Healer understands those cries and is touched with the feelings of those children.

This was the beginning of a profound healing in Betty's life. However, I wanted her to experience the ultimate wholeness promised in Romans 8:28. So we talked about trying to understand the meaning of her life. Where was God when she began life itself?

Had she made peace with the circumstances of her birth through an unwanted pregnancy? She said she hadn't.

I felt led to give her a strange assignment, one I've given out only a few times in all my counseling years. I said, "Betty, I am going to give you some homework and I want you to spend time meditating and praying about it. I want you to imagine the very moment of your conception. Imagine that particular time when one cell of life from your father broke into the living cell of your mother, and *you* came into existence. That's when *you* broke into human history. As you think about that, ask yourself one question: *where was God at that moment?*"

Betty took her assignment seriously. When we met one week later, she told me what had happened: "You know, the first two or three days, I really thought this whole thing was crazy. The only thing I could think of was a verse of Scripture which kept coming to my mind, 'In sin did my mother conceive me.' But about the third day when I was reluctantly meditating on it, I began to cry. But it was a different cry than usual. A prayer was welling up from way down inside me, and I wrote it down."

She handed it to me, and with her permission I share it with you:

O God, my heart leaps with the thought that You, my loving Father, have never forsaken me. You were there when I was conceived in earthly lust. You looked upon me with a Father's love even then. You were thinking of me in my mother's womb, planning in Your divine knowledge the person I was to become, molding me in Your image.

Knowing the pain in store, You gave me a mind that would pull me above the hurt, until in Your own timing You could heal me.

You were there when my mother gave birth to me, looking on in tenderness, standing in the vacant place of my father. You were there when I cried the bitter tears of a child whose father has abandoned her. You were holding me in Your arms all the while, rocking me gently in Your soothing love.

Oh, why did I not know of Your presence? Even as a child I was blind to Your love, unable to know it in its depth and breadth.

God, my dear, dear Father, my heart had turned to frost, but the light of Your love is beginning to warm it. I can feel again. You have begun to work in me a healing miracle. I trust You and I praise You. Your goodness and mercy have been with me always. Your love has never left me. And now the eyes of my soul have been opened. I see You for who You really are, my true Father. I know Your love and now I am ready to forgive. Please make the healing complete.

Betty had found the final stage of healing, when God took all the hurts she gave Him and healed them by His recycling and healing love. But then God put the frosting on the cake—He used Betty as a healed helper.

One Sunday morning I did something in my sermon I rarely do. With Betty's express permission I used the above story. I disguised details that would identify her, since I knew she would be in the congregation. At the end of the service I invited people to come forward to the front altar if they desired prayer for emotional healing. A large number responded. Betty was seated next to a friend who began to weep profusely during the time of invitation, but who did not go forward. Betty moved closer, and putting her arm around her friend, asked if she would like her to go with her and pray for her. The lady was hesitant, and protested that her problems were too deep and that Betty wouldn't really understand.

Now there took place within Betty a real struggle: she knew what she *thought* God was asking her to do, and she thought He was asking a little too much! But within minutes she knew what she had to do. So she leaned over and whispered in her friend's ear, "Don't be shocked: I gave Dr. Seamands permission to tell that story this morning: you see, *I'm Betty!*" Her friend looked at her incredulously.

"Yes," she said again, "I'm Betty, and I think I can understand and maybe help." They came forward together and spent a long time sharing and praying. This was the beginning of a healing in the life of Betty's friend. When Betty related it to me, she had the glow of a healed helper. God had truly recycled her hurts into healing and helpfulness!

PERSONAL REFLECTION

■ With what part of Betty's story do you most closely relate? Why? What encouragement, strength, and hope do you gain as the result of reading her story?

_____

_____

_____

_____

_____

_____

Too many of us think that we can only minister out of strength—that only when we are victorious and can impress people with our strong points will we bring God the most glory. But Paul claimed that there are only two things we can glory in. The first is the cross of Christ (Gal. 6:14), perhaps the ultimate place of weakness in all human history, the last word in injustice, which God turned into the salvation of the whole world. The other thing in which we can glory is our infirmities, or weaknesses (2 Cor. 12:9-10). Why? Because God's strength is made perfect in our weakness. As Christians we are called to be healed helpers, moving not out of strength, but out of weakness.

Often in the counseling room someone will share very deep problems or perplexities. There is always the temptation to impress him, to be the wise counselor, to move from strength and give good advice.

But then the Holy Spirit whispers, "David share *yourself* with this person. This is not a 'client,' not a 'case' (I hate that term!); this is a hurting human being. Let him in on your infirmities, your damaged emotions, and your struggles. Share with him how the Spirit has helped you in your weaknesses."

Often I inwardly resist and argue with the Spirit: "But Lord, I can't do that, because he has come to me as the pastor. He respects me; he sees me as strong and wise and having all the answers."

In time, I usually yield to His gentle pressure and follow His instructions. And every time I do, this promise of 2 Corinthinans 12:9-10 comes alive, as God has a chance to exercise His power, and as His strength is made perfect in and through my weakness.

Again and again I have been a part of this deep healing as God recycles the damages, the pains, and the infirmities and then uses them for someone's good and His glory.

What I have experienced in my own life, I have seen take place in the lives of many others. I dare to believe it can also happen in your life!

PERSONAL
REFLECTION

■ What, if any, reservations do you feel about sharing *yourself* (your failures, weaknesses, hurts, and pains of the past) with other people who could be helped by what you share? Why?

_____

_____

_____

_____

_____

■ What would you like to see God do *through* you in the lives of other people as the result of the healing work He's doing in your life?

_____

_____

_____

_____

_____

_____

_____

PRAYERFUL
REFLECTION

■ Go back and reread Betty's prayer. Underline or highlight any phrases that trigger a response from deep inside you. Then as a final journaling exercise, write a prayer expressing to God—just as Betty did—your deepest heart cries. Ask the Holy Spirit to help you get in touch with any feelings from the past that keep you stuck there. *NOTE: If you are counseling with a Christian therapist, or any other trained mental health care professional, you may choose to complete this writing exercise under his or her direction.*

_____

_____

_____

_____

_____

_____

_____

_____

_____

PERSONAL RENEWAL

■ As you continue your healing journey beyond this 13-week course, keep in mind what Paul told his Christian friends in Philippi (Phil. 1:6, NIV):

> *Being confident of this, that He who began a good work in you will carry it on to completion until the day of Jesus Christ.*

PART TWO

APPENDIX ONE

GROUP STUDY FORMAT

This workbook is designed for use both by individuals or in various group settings—such as support groups, Bible studies, or Sunday School classes.

Allow a minimum of 13 weeks for group study, focusing on one chapter of the book a week. Limit the length of each meeting to two hours.

How to Get a Group Started

Probably the best place to begin is by contacting the pastor of your church and letting him know of your interest in starting a support group using *Healing for Damaged Emotions* as the basis of your study. Tell him why you feel a study of this nature would be valuable to the members of the church and also how it can serve as an outreach to the community. Once you have acquired the necessary approval, find a meeting location and establish a date and time to begin the group.

A word about your meeting place. It should be a neutral setting rather than someone's home, if possible. Homes are often full of distractions (e.g., children, telephone calls). It is difficult to maintain an environment of strict confidentiality when family members are home. A room in the church can actually provide one of the safest places for your group to meet.

The next step is to get the word out about your group. You should be able to fill a group quickly by running an ad in your church bulletin and in the church activities section of your local newspaper. Ideally, your group should have six to twelve members, but start with fewer if necessary. In time, a support group that is working right will promote itself and you will not lack for group participants.

Meeting Format for Week 1 ONLY

1. Start on time. Welcome people as they arrive and make sure each person has a copy of the *Healing for Damaged Emotions Workbook*. Provide beverages if you wish. Ask everyone to complete and wear a name tag during your first meeting.

SPECIAL NOTE: Group participants should be asked to purchase their own copy of *Healing for Damaged Emotions Workbook* from a local Christian bookstore. Or, for the convenience of those who attend, you (the sponsoring church/organization) may choose to purchase a quantity of the books ahead of time and let group members buy them back from you at your first meeting.

2. Introduce yourself as the person who ran the ad. Explain that you would like the group to be a source of support for yourself and everyone present. Also let everyone know that the group is designed as a 13-week program, including this first meeting.

3. Explain that leadership will rotate within the group so that each week a different member will lead the group. It is the responsibility of the person leading to start the meeting on time, remind group members of the writing assignment for the following week, and to find another leader for the following week, prior to closing the meeting.

4. Emphasize that everything that is said during the meeting is to remain in the meeting, that none of what is shared should be discussed outside the group. This is *crucial* to the effectiveness of the program.

5. Explain that it would be helpful for everyone to hear one another's reasons for coming to the group and invite each person to take up to five minutes to talk about what made him or her decide to attend. Let group participants know that no one has to talk for that long, but that this amount of time is available for anyone who wants it. Volunteer to begin by giving your name and briefly telling your own story.

6. Ask group members to turn to the Personal Journey Summary Sheet for Week 1 on page 201. Explain that the basic format for each meeting will be that of a writing workshop. Group members will be asked to write down their response to each of the questions listed on the page for that week. They will normally be given fifteen minutes to do their writing. A three-minute warning prior to the end of the writing time will be given to let group members know they should be writing their answer for the final question on the page.

7. Ask group members to take ten minutes at this point to complete their writing for the Personal Journey Summary Sheet, Week 1. Give a three-minute warning prior to the end of the writing time.

8. Go around the group and have each person read what he or she has written for *only* the last question on the sheet. Anyone may "pass" if they do *not* wish to answer the question, but encourage as many as possible to participate.

9. Discuss the Guidelines for Group Sharing which are spelled out on page 200.

10. Ask if anyone has a prayer request regarding themselves or others. Note those requests, then close in prayer for the group.

11. Ask if someone would be willing to lead the group the following week.

12. Remind group members to read and work the journaling exercises in Chapter 1 for the following week.

Meeting Format for Weeks 2–13

1. Welcome everyone. Have first-time visitors introduce themselves by name.

2. Ask group members to join you for a moment of silent prayer. Encourage everyone to focus their thoughts and open their hearts and minds to what the Holy Spirit wants to say to them during this week's discussion.

3. Have group members turn to the Personal Journey Summary Sheet for the week and spend fifteen minutes writing down their response to each of the questions listed on the page. Give a three-minute warning prior to the end of the writing time.

4. If there are more than ten of you present at your meeting, split into smaller groups of five or six each for Family Group Sharing (described in the next step).

5. Family Group Sharing: Designate one person in each group as the lead reader. This means that that person begins the time of sharing by reading his or her answer to the first question on the page. Then proceeding around the circle, everyone in the group may take a turn reading what he or she has written for that question. IMPORTANT NOTE: Anyone in a family group may "pass" if he or she does *not* wish to read his or her answer to the question. Repeat this same process for each of the questions on the page. Before breaking into family groups, review these simple rules for sharing (see the next step).

6. Rules for Family Group Sharing: ■ Allow equal time for each family member to share; ■ Please limit individual sharing to explanations of the written material; ■ Feedback from family members may be offered only after every person in the family group has had an opportunity to share what he or she has written for the question being answered.

7. Reassemble the whole group after approximately 60 minutes. Ask if anyone would like to share anything from their reading and writing experience during the week, or something they learned during this week's Family Group Sharing time.

8. Spend the last 15 minutes of your meeting in prayer. Ask if anyone wants to share a prayer request regarding themselves or others. Then pray for one another.

9. Let group members know what the reading and writing assignment is for the following week. Encourage everyone to complete that work prior to coming to the next week's meeting.

10. Ask if someone would be willing to lead the group the following week.

GUIDELINES FOR GROUP SHARING

Each person heals from damaged emotions at a different pace. But everyone's healing process is enhanced by the mutual support and encouragement that is found in a group setting. The following guidelines will help keep the group process healthy. Take time to read these guidelines aloud at each session, if necessary, as a reminder of the way the group process should work.

Group Guidelines

1. Remember that trust grows over time. Share only as much as what feels safe for you. Risk sharing more when you feel safe doing so.

2. Be an attentive listener. You can learn much from other people's insights if you will take time to really hear what they are saying.

3. Maintain confidences. Remember that anything that is said in the group is considered confidential and must **not** be shared outside the group unless specific permission is given to do so. Memorize this rule: WHO YOU SEE HERE, WHAT IS SAID HERE, WHEN YOU LEAVE HERE, LET IT STAY HERE. This is *crucial* to the effectiveness of this program.

4. Limit your sharing to what is written on your summary sheet. This will allow everyone in the group who wishes to share the opportunity to do so.

5. Talk only about yourself and your own situation. Avoid getting into conversations that focus on other people (including your spouse, children, friends, etc.).

6. Avoid giving advice. Everyone is welcome to share their personal experience and what has worked for them in the healing process, but no one is to advise another person about what he or she should do.

7. No cross-talk. Cross-talk is when two people engage in a conversation that excludes the other members of the group. Speak only when it is your turn.

8. Be as honest with yourself and others as you possibly can be. Pray for the other members of the group. Remember what James tells us: "Confess your sins to one another and pray for each other so God can heal you" (James 5:16, NCV).

PERSONAL JOURNEY SUMMARY SHEET
"Telling My Story"

MEETING FOCUS: The best way to begin is to share your story, because doing so will forge an immediate bond and foster a sense of belonging.

■ What made you decide to come to this group? Briefly describe what has been happening in your life that makes the topic of "healing for damaged emotions" relevant to your life.

_____

_____

_____

_____

_____

_____

■ What was your family like as you were growing up? How did your parents relate to each other? How did they relate to you? Did you have brothers and sisters? How did you and your siblings get along?

_____

_____

_____

_____

_____

■ Would you describe yourself as a person who is "in touch" with your feelings? Why? What, if any, feelings are difficult for you to express?

_____

_____

_____

_____

■ What would you like to see God do in your life as the result of going through this workbook, *Healing for Damaged Emotions*?

_____

_____

_____

_____

PERSONAL JOURNEY SUMMARY SHEET
Chapter 1—Damaged Emotions

MEETING FOCUS: Being a Christian doesn't mean you will automatically be healed of all the emotional damage done in the past.

■ What problem areas of your life have persisted—in spite of godly advice you've received, Scriptures you've read, or prayers you've prayed to God? Briefly describe your struggle.

_____

_____

_____

_____

_____

■ What do you most fear about having to get in touch with the pain of your past?

_____

_____

_____

_____

_____

■ Dr. Seamands lists five frequently damaged emotions people struggle with—*inferiority, perfectionism, supersensitivity, fear,* and *sex.* Of these five emotional areas, which one do you struggle with the most? Describe a recent situation where you found yourself dealing with one of these five feeling areas.

_____

_____

_____

_____

_____

_____

_____

■ How are you feeling right now about letting the Holy Spirit "tinker" in your life at an emotional level? Write out your response in the form of a short sentence prayer to God.

_____

_____

_____

_____

_____

PERSONAL JOURNEY SUMMARY SHEET
Chapter 2—Guilt, Grace, and Debt-Collecting

MEETING FOCUS: Only after you have accepted God's unconditional forgiveness are you set free to forgive others.

■ Describe a time when you needed to be forgiven. Did you seek forgiveness in that situation? What happened in your life as the result of seeking forgiveness?

_____

_____

_____

_____

■ If forgiveness is "the act of setting someone free from the obligation to pay for the wrong that has been done against you," then can you think of anyone in your life at present who you still need to forgive? What keeps you from pardoning that person? What are some steps you may need to take to get to the point of forgiving him or her?

_____

_____

_____

_____

_____

■ Your failure to *see* and *know* and *feel* God's grace in your life may already have driven you to the tragic treadmill of performing, achieving, and striving. In what ways has your relationship with Christ been based on the DO and DON'T DO messages communicated by the church or other Christians?

_____

_____

_____

_____

_____

■ What insights did you gain about yourself, forgiveness and God this week as the result of working the material in Chapter 2? What steps might you need to take to experience more of the kind of forgiveness talked about in this week's material?

_____

_____

_____

_____

_____

_____

PERSONAL JOURNEY SUMMARY SHEET
Chapter 3—The Wounded Healer

MEETING FOCUS: Because of what Jesus suffered emotionally in His humanity, you can be certain that God knows, cares, and fully understands your feelings of woundedness.

■ Dr. Seamands describes the biblical term *infirmities* as "crippling weaknesses that sabotage our happiness and relationships and keep us from taking responsibility for our own lives." List any "infirmities" in your life of which you are aware.

_____

_____

_____

_____

■ Can you recall any instances in your life when someone provided an understanding ear and unusual empathy in relation to a painful situation you were going through at that point in time? How did it make you feel knowing that person understood and cared?

_____

_____

_____

_____

■ Jesus experienced many painful moments while He lived among men. For this reason, He is ever sensitive and fully compassionate toward us who experience the pain of rejection, loss, depression, loneliness, fear and ever so many other feelings. How does knowing this about Jesus make a difference in your life right now?

_____

_____

_____

_____

_____

_____

■ During the past week, what insights did you gain as the result of working through the material in this book?

_____

_____

_____

_____

_____

_____

PERSONAL JOURNEY SUMMARY SHEET
Chapter 4—Satan's Deadliest Weapon

MEETING FOCUS: Low self-esteem is Satan's deadliest psychological weapon, and it can keep you going around in vicious circles of fear and uselessness.

■ Of the seven deadly psychological weapons Satan uses to defeat us—fear, doubt, anger, hostility, worry, guilt, low self-esteem—which one(s) has he used in your life most often to cause you to feel defeated? Give an example or two.

_____

_____

_____

_____

_____

■ How would you rate your own level of self-esteem? Too low? Too high? Appropriate? Describe you as you see yourself today.

_____

_____

_____

_____

■ Describe situations that trigger your sense of feeling less than other people and the thinking that accompanies those feelings.

_____

_____

_____

_____

_____

_____

_____

■ You are seen by God as being so precious that you are infinite in worth. Complete the following prayer, putting into words your feelings about God's unconditional acceptance of you.

Dear Lord Jesus,

Knowing You value me so much _____

_____

_____

_____

_____

_____

_____

PERSONAL JOURNEY SUMMARY SHEET
Chapter 5—Healing Our Low Self-Esteem—Part One

MEETING FOCUS: How you see and feel about yourself affects your relationships with God, yourself, and others.

- In his book *The Sensation of Being Somebody*, Dr. Maurice Wagner explains the three essential components of a healthy self-image:

  A sense of belongingness — "I am wanted, accepted, cared for, enjoyed and loved."

  A sense of worthwhileness — "I count. I am of value. I have something to offer."

  A sense of competence — "I can do this task. I can cope with that situation. I am able to meet life."

  Of the three components of a healthy self-image listed above, which one do you seem to wrestle with the most? Give an example of how one of these three components is negatively affecting your life at present.

  _____

  _____

  _____

  _____

- The mirror of life gives us certain reflections and images which influence how we see and feel about ourselves. Who or what most influenced how you see yourself today? Would you say you have an accurate or a distorted view of who you are today? Explain.

  _____

  _____

_____

_____

_____

■ In what ways has a distorted self-image adversely affected your relationship with God? With other people? Describe specific struggles you've faced because you have an inaccurate picture of yourself.

_____

_____

_____

_____

_____

■ Does knowing that you are "a child of God" make a difference in how you see yourself? Why? What steps might you need to take to get a more realistic picture of who you are as a child of God?

_____

_____

_____

_____

PERSONAL JOURNEY SUMMARY SHEET
Chapter 6—Healing Our Low Self-Esteem—Part Two

MEETING FOCUS: Proper self-love is the only sure foundation on which to build loving relationships with other people.

■ What comes to mind when you hear the term *self-love?* Describe what self-love looks like to you.

_____

_____

_____

_____

_____

■ In Philippians 2:3, the Apostle Paul writes, "Do nothing out of selfish ambition or vain conceit, but in humility consider others better than yourselves." What is your understanding of this verse? Have you been taught that to stay humble you have to dislike yourself? How has this kind of thinking impacted your ability to love yourself? Your ability to love God?

_____

_____

_____

_____

■ What are some things you do to nurture or love yourself? How has proper self-nurturing made a difference in your ability to "love your neighbor (your spouse, children, friend, employer) as yourself"? What happens when you don't properly nurture yourself?

_____

_____

_____

_____

_____

_____

■ God often loves us through other people. Cite specific instances in the past week or two when God used other people in your life to show you how much He loves, affirms, and accepts you.

_____

_____

_____

_____

_____

_____

PERSONAL JOURNEY SUMMARY SHEET
Chapter 7—Symptoms of Perfectionism

MEETING FOCUS: Perfectionism will lead you as a Christian to endless striving to please a false god.

■ How many times did you catch yourself this week using the phrases, "could have," "should have," "would have," or "if only." List a few examples.

_____

_____

_____

_____

_____

■ What behaviors in your life might indicate that you are holding on to a subtle belief that God is a "relentless taskmaster"—that no matter how much you do or how well you do it, it will never quite be enough to keep Him happy?

_____

_____

_____

_____

_____

_____

■ Dr. Seamands states, " . . . the way to God is not the path of perfect performance." In what ways have you been living out your Christianity by adhering to the do's and don'ts spelled out by the churches you've attended or the Christians you've known?

_____

_____

_____

_____

_____

■ The healing of perfectionism takes place on a day-to-day basis as you realize and accept God's grace (His freely given, unearnable kindness and favor) in your life. Describe specific ways you've experienced God's grace in your life recently? How do those experiences make you feel about your relationship with God?

_____

_____

_____

_____

_____

_____

PERSONAL JOURNEY SUMMARY SHEET
Chapter 8—The Process of Healing for Perfectionism

MEETING FOCUS: Healing for perfectionism is a process. It involves growing in grace, reprogramming, and healing in every level of your life.

■ Emotional healing is a process. Submitting to the process is the first step. Have you taken the first step? What motivates you to see this process through to the end?

_____

_____

_____

_____

■ *Unpleaseable parents* and *unpredictable home situations* are two of the root causes of perfectionism. In what ways did these two influences breed perfectionism in you? Describe one situation from your childhood which illustrates the unpleaseable nature of your parents and one situation that shows your home situation as being unpredictable.

_____

_____

_____

_____

■ The healing process touches various levels of a person's life. As God's grace works in these areas of your life and applies positive assurance of hope and help through His grace, you begin to find growth and freedom.

217

Of the five areas of emotional healing listed below, from which two are you *most needing* to be healed?

■ The mind—distorted concepts
■ The feelings—damaged emotions
■ Perceptions—downgrading evaluations
■ Relationships—disruptive contradictions
■ Memories—Past hurts that replay in the present and interfere with the way you live

■ Hidden anger is another byproduct of damaged emotions. What anger and resentment did you uncover this week as the result of doing the writing exercises in the book? Briefly describe one or two.

_____

_____

_____

_____

■ Dr. Seamands states, "There is *nothing* you can share out of the agonizing hurts and depths and hates and rages of your soul that God has not heard. There is *nothing* you take to Him that He will not understand. He will receive you with love and grace." Is there anything you are longing to express to God right now? Do so in the form of a prayer. He will understand and receive you with love and grace.

_____

_____

_____

_____

PERSONAL JOURNEY SUMMARY SHEET
Chapter 9—Super You or Real You?

MEETING FOCUS: God wants to heal you and change you in order that Real You can become the person He created you to be.

■ Super You is a false, idealized image you think you have to be in order to be loved and accepted. In what ways have you changed your outer self (the way you look, act, think, and feel) in order to gain other people's love and acceptance?

_____

_____

_____

_____

_____

■ The term *inner child* is a popular phrase used in recovery circles today. Your inner child has been described as "a composite of your feelings, your natural talents, and the unique dimensions of your personality." According to this definition, describe in two or three sentences what you know about your inner child. (Your inner child is the Real You!)

_____

_____

_____

_____

_____

_____

_____

■ Super You denies legitimate emotions that need fair and proper
expression. What were you taught about *anger, conflict,* and
happiness? How have you handled these three emotions in your
life? Note specific instances in your life when you either freely
expressed or felt compelled to repress those feelings.

_____

_____

_____

_____

_____

■ The *only you* that God really knows and sees is the Real You. In
what ways have you robbed yourself of spiritual and emotional
growth and the friendship of God by trying to keep the Real You
hidden from God and other people? Are you ready to let God
accept and *love* the Real You? Tell Him so by writing a short prayer
below.

_____

_____

_____

_____

PERSONAL JOURNEY SUMMARY SHEET
Chapter 10—Myths and Truths about Depression

MEETING FOCUS: As a Christian you will experience depression. Do not view it as spiritual failure, but simply as a normal part of life.

■ Describe a time when you felt depressed. What brought about the depression? How did you deal with it? And how did other people around you respond to it?

_____

_____

_____

_____

_____

_____

■ When do you most often feel depressed? Make a list of things which seem to bring about depression in your life.

_____

_____

_____

_____

_____

_____

■ One of Satan's tricks is to take your depression and turn it into spiritual defeat, doubt, and despondency. Describe a time when you found yourself feeling depressed and, consequently, spiritually defeated.

_____

_____

_____

_____

_____

_____

■ What is your personal strategy for overcoming depression? What part do thanksgiving and praise play in your strategy?

_____

_____

_____

_____

_____

_____

■ If you want to, share the "Song of Praise" you wrote as part of your homework assignment for this week.

PERSONAL JOURNEY SUMMARY SHEET
Chapter 11—Dealing with Depression

MEETING FOCUS: As you admit and examine your depression, you can go on to take positive steps toward healing.

■ What physical, emotional, or spiritual limits have you been exceeding lately? What did you discover during the week as you inventoried your life in these three areas? Briefly summarize what you discovered.

_____

_____

_____

_____

_____

■ Injustice is just one of three primary reactions that leads to depression. Often, injustice is rooted in early childhood experiences, which later in life, if unidentified and left undealt with, leads to bitterness and resentment. What roots of bitterness or key resentments did you identify this week as you worked through the material in the book? Describe a few of them. How have those resentments affected your life?

_____

_____

_____

_____

_____

_____

■ How have you overcome depression in the past? Which of the practical suggestions for dealing with depression that Dr. Seamands touches on in Chapter 11 did you like the best? Why?

_____

_____

_____

_____

_____

■ Jesus has given you the Holy Spirit—the *Paraclete*. He is "the One called alongside" who is ALWAYS with you. Describe your experience with the Holy Spirit as the Paraclete. How has He come alongside and helped you during times of depression? How easy was it for you to depend on Him for the comfort He promises during times of discomfort? Why?

_____

_____

_____

_____

_____

PERSONAL JOURNEY SUMMARY SHEET
Chapter 12—Healed Helpers

MEETING FOCUS: God can take the healing process of your life and use it to help others find healing in their lives.

- Describe a time when the Holy Spirit searched your heart (subconscious mind) and brought to light a deep hurt or pain in you that needed to be healed. What was the result of Him revealing that truth to you about your own brokenness?

  _____

  _____

  _____

  _____

  _____

- In what ways have the hurts of your past cultivated in your heart more compassion for others who have experienced similar hurts?

  _____

  _____

  _____

- Dr. Seamands reminds us that the greatest miracle in the healing of damaged emotions is that God "can change hurtful insights to helpful outreach." How have you experienced this in your own life? Recount a specific instance when you saw God use your healing process to help someone else find healing in his or her life.

  _____

  _____

_____

_____

- What, if any, reservations do you feel about sharing *yourself* (your failures, weaknesses, hurts, and pains of the past) with other people who could be helped by what you share? Why?

_____

_____

_____

- Take just a minute to reflect back over the past twelve weeks of this course. Have you had a clear sense that God's purposes were being fulfilled in your life as you struggled through the issues related to your own healing process? Briefly describe the personal benefits of being involved in this course over the past twelve weeks.

_____

_____

_____

_____

- *(Optional)* Share with the other members of your group the "Master Weaver's Work of Art" piece you did as part of this week's homework assignment.

Appendix Two

Support Group Resources

CHRISTIAN RESOURCES

Alcoholics for Christ, Inc.
1316 North Campbell Road
Royal Oak, MI 48067
(313) 399-9955

Alcoholics Victorious
International Service Office
1700 Eighth Street
Lewiston, ID 83501

Christian Alcoholics
Rehabilitation Association
FOA Road
Pocahontas, MS 39072

Exodus International
P.O. Box 2121
San Rafael, CA 94912
(415) 454-1017

Institute for Christian Living
Riverside Medical Center
Minneapolis, MN 55427
(612) 593-1791

Liontamers
2801 North Brea Blvd.
Fullerton, CA 92635-2799

Minirth-Meier Clinic West
260 Newport Center Drive #430
Newport Beach, CA 92660
(800) 877-HOPE

**National Association for
Christian Recovery**
P.O. Box 11095
Whittier, CA 90603
(213) 697-6201

New Life Treatment Centers
570 Glenneyre, Suite 107
Laguna Beach, CA 92651
(800) 227-LIFE

Overcomers Outreach, Inc.
2290 West Whittier Blvd.
La Habra, CA 90631
(213) 697-3994

Tools for Recovery
1201 Knoxville Street
San Diego, CA 92110-3718
(800) 873-8384

SECULAR RESOURCES

Adult Children of Alcoholics
Central Service Board
P.O. Box 35623
Los Angeles, CA 90035
(213) 464-4423

Alcoholics Anonymous
P.O. Box 459
Grand Central Station
New York, NY 10163
(212) 686-1100

Al-Anon/Alateen
Family Group Headquarters, Inc.
P.O. Box 182
Madison Square Station
New York, NY 10159
(800) 344-2666
(212) 302-7240

Codependents Anonymous
P.O. Box 33577
Phoenix, AZ 85067-3577
(602) 944-1141

Debtors Anonymous
314 West 53rd Street
New York, NY 10018
(212) 969-0710

Emotions Anonymous
P.O. Box 4245
St. Paul, MN 55104
(612) 647-9712

Gamblers Anonymous
P.O. Box 17173
Los Angeles, CA 90017
(213) 386-8769

Incest Survivors Anonymous
P.O. Box 5613
Long Beach, CA 90800

Narcotics Anonymous
World Service Office
16155 Wyandotte Street
Van Nuys, CA 91406
(818) 780-3951

Overeaters Anonymous
World Service Office
2190 190th Street
Torrance, CA 90504
(213) 320-7941

Sex Addicts Anonymous
P.O. Box 3038
Minneapolis, MN 55403
(612) 871-1520

Sex & Love Addicts Anonymous
P.O. Box 119
Boston, MA 02258

Specialized Reading Resources

BOOKS RELATED TO FAMILY SYSTEMS

- Stephen Arterburn and David Stoop, *The Angry Man* (Waco, Texas: Word Books), 1991.
- John Bradshaw, *Bradshaw On: The Family* (Deerfield Beach, Florida: Health Communications, Inc.), 1988.
- Rich Buhler, *Love: No Strings Attached* (Nashville: Thomas Nelson Publications), 1987.
- Dave Carder, Earl Henslin, John Townsend, Henry Cloud and Alice Brawand, *Secrets of Your Family Tree* (Chicago: Moody Press), 1991.
- Gary Smalley and John Trent, *Love Is a Decision* (Waco, Texas: Word Books), 1989.
- David Stoop and James Masteller, *Forgiving Our Parents, Forgiving Ourselves* (Ann Arbor, Michigan: Servant Publications), 1992.

BOOKS RELATED TO CODEPENDENCE

- Melody Beattie, *Codependent No More* (New York: Hazelden/Harper), 1987.
- Alfred Ells, *One-Way Relationships* (Nashville: Thomas Nelson Publications), 1990.
- Robert Hemfelt, Frank Minirth and Paul Meier, *Love Is a Choice* (Nashville: Thomas Nelson Publications), 1989.
- Robert S. McGee, *The Search for Significance* (Houston: Rapha Publishing), 1990.
- Pia Mellody, *Facing Codependence* (San Francisco: Harper & Row), 1989.

BOOKS RELATED TO ADULT CHILDREN

- William Backus and Marie Chapian, *Telling Yourself the Truth* (Minneapolis: Bethany House), 1980.
- John Bradshaw, *Healing the Shame That Binds You* (Deerfield Beach, Florida: Health Communications, Inc.), 1988.
- Henry Cloud, *When Your World Makes No Sense* (Nashville: Thomas Nelson Publications), 1990.

- Jim Conway, *Adult Children of Legal or Emotional Divorce* (Downers Grove, Illinois: InterVarsity Press), 1990.
- Richard W. Dickinson and Carol Gift Page, *The Child in Each of Us* (Wheaton, Illinois: Victor Books), 1989.
- Ron Ross, *When I Grow Up . . .* (San Diego: Recovery Publications, Inc.), 1990.
- David Seamands, *Putting Away Childish Things* (Wheaton, Illinois: Victor Books), 1982.
- Charles Sell, *Unfinished Business* (Portland, Oregon: Multnomah Press), 1989.

BOOKS RELATED TO ADDICTION

- Stephen Arterburn, *Addicted to "Love"* (Ann Arbor, Michigan: Servant Publications), 1991.
- Howard Halpern, *How to Break Your Addiction to a Person* (New York: Bantam Books), 1982.
- David Johnson and Jeff Van Vonderen, *The Subtle Power of Spiritual Abuse* (Minneapolis: Bethany House), 1991.
- Grant Martin, *When Good Things Become Addictions* (Wheaton, Illinois: Victor Books), 1990.
- Gerald May, *Addiction and Grace* (New York: Harper & Row), 1988.

BOOKS RELATED TO THE 12-STEP PROCESS

- Friends in Recovery, *The Twelve Steps—A Spiritual Journey* (San Diego: Recovery Publications, Inc.), 1988.
- Keith Miller, *A Hunger for Healing* (San Francisco: Harper & Row), 1991.

APPENDIX THREE

SUPPLEMENTAL JOURNALING PAGES

The Lord is gracious and compassionate, slow to anger and rich in love.
PSALM 103:8

All the days ordained for me were written in Your book before one of them came to be. PSALM 139:16

Be kind and compassionate to one another, forgiving each other, just as in Christ God forgave you. EPHESIANS 4:32

The Lord is . . . a stonghold in times of trouble.
PSALM 9:9

I know the plans I have for you . . . plans to give you hope and a future. JEREMIAH 29:11